THEM GOON RULES

THEM GOON RULES

FUGITIVE ESSAYS ON RADICAL BLACK FEMINISM

MARQUIS BEY

THE UNIVERSITY OF
ARIZONA PRESS
TUCSON

The University of Arizona Press
www.uapress.arizona.edu

ISBN-13: 978-0-8165-3943-7 (paper)

Cover design by Leigh McDonald
Cover art: *Black Interiority* by Torkwase Dyson

Publication of this book is made possible in part by the proceeds of a permanent
endowment created with the assistance of a Challenge Grant from the National
Endowment for the Humanities, a federal agency.

Library of Congress Cataloging-in-Publication Data
Names: Bey, Marquis, author.
Title: Them goon rules : fugitive essays on radical Black feminism / Marquis Bey.
Description: Tucson : The University of Arizona Press, 2019 | Series: The Feminist wire books:
     connecting feminisms, race and social justice | Includes bibliographical references.
Identifiers: LCCN 2018038443 | ISBN 9780816539437 (pbk. : alk. paper)
Subjects: LCSH: Feminism—United States. | Blacks—Race identity. | African American
     feminists—History. | Queer theory. | Gender identity. | LCGFT: Essays.
Classification: LCC HQ1410 .B49 2019 | DDC 305.420973—dc23 LC record available at
     https://lccn.loc.gov/2018038443

Printed in the United States of America
♾ This paper meets the requirements of ANSI/NISO Z39.48-1992 (Permanence of Paper).

To Danny, my beloved comrade, living and loving in the trenches with me.

"Blackness"[:] *a symbolic program of philosophical "disobedi-ence" (a systematic skepticism and refusal) that would make the former available to* anyone, *or more pointedly,* any *posture, that was willing to take on the formidable task of* thinking *as a willful act of imagination and invention.*

— Hortense Spillers, "Peter's Pans: Eating in the Diaspora"

Fugitivity is seeing around corners, stockpiling in crevices, knowing the "unrules," being unruly, because the rules are never enough, and not even close.

— Keguro Macharia, "Fugitivity"

CONTENTS

PREFACE

I came to the thoughts herein by way of much struggle. At times I'm not even sure I believe myself, but concomitant with that uncertainty is an insistence on rigorous thought and, despite discursive timidity, *parrhesia*—bold, fierce, unfettered speech. I do not know if the thoughts here are cogent; I do not know if they will serve the nebulous "revolution" or if they are mere elitist musings that surrender to an increasingly arcane mode of thinking masquerading as radical. Ever the votary of Socrates—he was, after all, one of my first intellectual loves, one who has subsequently been brought to the dark side, the Black-hand side, as it were—I concede only that I know nothing. I can only insist persistently that these fugitive musings on the Blackness of it all, the Black feminism of it all, the queerness of it all, are in the interest of saying things that have long been said but saying them differently, in hopes that some of y'all might get on board with this stuff that's been circulating for a while now in clandestine enclaves and subterranean juke joints. I am nothing but a thief stealing shit I vibe with from others and making it do a different kind of work. Hacking already hacked ideas, stealing stolen things and giving them away so others can steal more things. It is an expansive dispersal and unowning of fugitive knowledge that I want you, all of you, to be down with. Though I pilfer, it is all in a coalitional interest that does not forsake the rebellious underpinnings of my source material. I am a thief, mind you, because I am born of thieves.

The fugitivity of these essays lies in their discursive folds and syntactical gaps laced with Black studies (the study of that force we have come to call Blackness), feminist theory (the hieroglyphic attention to the breakdowns of doing—and doing again, and doing wrongly, badly—gender), and queer studies (the fuzzy *khōra*, in the Derridean sense, that fractures communicability by engendering the salvific effects of the nonnormative). The fugitivity of these essays lies in the troubling of origins, of expectant templates that exist ahead of themselves. Forgive my dogmatic insistence on existentialist doctrine, but I yearn for the coalitional self-determinative, the essence that comes after the disputed fact, or rather is held in abeyance, deferred. It is the fugitivity that I love, its escapeful curves, its troublesome elusiveness. I love the flight and its paradoxical hereness—flight that refuses by taking off without leaving behind. That is the language I have been bred in, the language that has produced the struggle that troubles me and will hopefully, if I am marginally successful, trouble you.

What has perhaps driven me most to write these thoughts and compile them for you—or, so very egotistically, for myself, to validate me in my pursuit of eluding pursuit—is a tendency to be animated by the word *refuse*. And indeed its double gesture is precisely the point: I am animated by refusal, by subversive *Nah*-ness, by that Melvillean scrivener's "I would prefer not to"; and, too, by the refuse, those who have been deemed disposable, debris, waste. I affiliate with the lineage of the thrown away, those whose existence was deemed antithetical to livability. I affiliate with problem people, which is to say possibility people, *im*possibility people, people who live where there is said to be no life to be lived. I affiliate with the ontologically criminalized so that we can engender insurgent forms of care work. They have all, however grittily and partially, escaped. And I want that. I want to mobilize around that penchant and yearning for escape. Not a cowardly going away but a subversive refusal of the tenets of legibility, of being read, clocked, eyed, peeped. A nonnormativity the essence of which is a dispersive refusal pregnant with the sonic resonances of the disruptively vibrating "lower frequencies." It is a fugitivity in all its connotative vibrancy that I find, not to the exclusion of other manifestations, in the Black and feminist and queer spaces that surround and subtend us in undercommon deviancy. They whisper to me, and to many others. I have tried to write the curvature of those whispers.

To close, then, I want to make a confession: I fear what these essays might do. I have made myself vulnerable in this discursive space. So, because of this, I fear that loved ones, friends, colleagues, strangers, acquaintances, you name 'em, will not recognize me in these pages. I fear that, when confronted with an unhinged and unshackled tongue—a fugitive tongue, if you will—they will reject me. I ask you humbly, then, though my words may strike you as uncharacteristic or harsh—perhaps even downright wrong, dangerous, out of touch, or silly—to know that I am speaking, oddly enough, from love, from integrity, and from the deep recesses of the mind that very few know. So take this as a timid gift of my thoughts, thoughts that often go unexpressed; take this as a diffident display of my vulnerability; take this as a discursive act of overwhelming love. Take it and do what you wish with it, I suppose, since the author, once their work is out of their hands, dies a little death. But please, I ask you: let it speak.

O! receive the fugitive. . . .[1]

— Marquis, Philadelphia 2018

ACKNOWLEDGMENTS

*To the extent that I said anything or that I have something to
say, that's because a whole bunch of people, a whole bunch of
history, a whole bunch of things sent me to say it.*

— Fred Moten, "An Interview with Fred Moten"

Y'all, I am immensely indebted to those who are and have been
in my life. Indeed, in both a literal and a proverbial sense, I
owe my life to them. All of it started, fundamentally, with my
mother, Toya; my grandmother Florence; my brother Gordon ("Gee");
my Aunts Lil and Landa; my Uncle Tommy; my cousin Marcus; and
even those little monsters, my sister Tianna ("TT") and my brother's
kid, Chase.

To my Cornell colleagues: Amaris Brown, Jessica Rodriguez, Ama
Bemma Adwetewa-Badu, Philippa Chun, Abram Coetsee, Mint Dam-
rongpiwat, Verdie Culbreath, Xine Yao, Nasrin Olla, Sadrach Pierre
(a vital interlocutor, to say the very least). To my graduate mentors:
Dagmawi Woubshet, Margo Natalie Crawford, C. Riley Snorton, La
Marr Jurelle Bruce. And to my incoming cohort: Chris Berardino,
Matt Kilbane, Kristen Angierski, Katie Thorsteinson, Liz M. Alexander, Gabriella Freidman, Brianna Thompson, Mariana Alarcón. And
to not mention my students would be an egregious oversight. I thank

all of them, especially Matija, Emma, Emmy, Lexi, Raven, Cat, Barr, Valery, Aaliyah, and Kyra.

My more recent upstate New York folks deserve special thanks too. Stacy, your riotous levity and humble exuberance is enjoyed, a balm for the proverbial soul. Steph, my feminist comrade, my feminist bibliophile loving the feminism of it all with me. Sri, your kindness, your word-nerdiness, your genuine care for those closest to you: a marvel. Kiera, Sunday night Catan phenom, the progenitor of "sven."

And my folks from PA: Jeff Robbins, Noelle Vahanian, Robert Valgenti, Cathy Romagnolo, Teddi Sakellarides, Kira Ianthe Silvanus (temporarily lost but found again, blessedly, in feminist solidarity). All of you, my first teachers in the formal sense of the word.

Some more extended shout-outs are in order as well. A very special thank-you to perhaps my closest colleague, friend, intellectual sparring partner, and, frankly, in the gritty and rigorous sense of Black thought, kin: Jesse Goldberg. Jesse, you have given me that Derridean gift that cannot, and does not ask to, be paid back. You have gifted me with your thoughts, your rigor, your tenacity. We have shared, and will continue to share, the love of thinking together. So that's all I can say: a thank-you that comes nowhere near repaying that intellectual and social debt that is not a debt.

Danny, to whom this collection is dedicated. I hope you know how immensely impactful you have been in my life. Your mischievousness has long been an inspiration for my burgeoning deviance, your intellectual fierceness something to be envied. We met way back, almost a decade ago now, and since then we have been forging family in the illustrious grime of the trenches. We live and love in the intellectual and political trenches, together, we and all our fierce philosophical people. But you were perhaps my first, and that is, as I am not wont to say but I'll say anyway, sacred.

And of course I could not thank anyone without thanking Kate. You have been integral, though recent, in my writerly life. Your vulnerability and patience, your levity and strategic seriousness have only been the greatest of benefits to me. (In addition to your refusal to pronounce the letter *r*.) Your support, your care, your indefatigable will—treasures I can only try to imitate, in awe of your perfection of the art. And you are, because of this and so many other things, loved. And I thank you, immensely.

Thank you to the Feminist Wire book series and their collaboration with the University of Arizona Press. Kristen, Monica, Tamura, Darnell: not only were you all integral to this book becoming, well, a book; you are all truly and unapologetically dope.

My thanks, too, to Public Humanities NY for providing the fellowship that allowed me to work with the Audre Lorde Project, without whom I would not have even conceptualized the essay "The ALP Journals" herein; and the donors of the Truman Capote PhD Writer's Award.

I am grateful, lastly, to *The Feminist Wire*, *The Coffeelicious*, and *RaceBaitR*, on which some of these essays first appeared in a less expanded form.

My authorship is always collaborative, and these are my collaborators. I am always writing from the inspiration, the force, of others. Without others, I could not write. So I guess with this, too, I should thank Fred Moten, for without him, without him sending me to say what I have said, I could not have written this. Dr. Moten—Fred, if I may—thank you for externalizing your language to me and, most importantly, staying a "black motherfucker."

THEM GOON RULES

UNRULY

What would it mean to think about blackness as that which experimentalizes being, that which . . . moves as unfettered ur-matter, unthinkable exorbitance, and deregulated transubstantiation? What is at stake when black flesh fugitively undulates into and as ether and, in so doing, un/makes the world itself? What might it mean to think about blackness as enacting an un/making, as enacting amid regimes of settlement an unsettling that is also an un/holding, a release of self from its entrapment within property into an alternate intimacy?

— J. Kameron Carter and Sarah Jane Cervenak, "Black Ether"

Whence We Are Sent

These people are my access to me; they are my entrance to my own interior life. Which is why the images that float around them—the remains, so to speak . . . surface first, and they surface so vividly and so compellingly that I acknowledge them as my route to a reconstruction of a world, to an exploration of an interior life that was not written and to the revelation of a kind of truth.

— Toni Morrison, "Site of Memory"

I was sent, tell that to history.

— Lorna Goodison, "Nanny"

f I am here, wherever here is, it is because I was sent here by folks who have been putting in work for a minute. I am here with them even if they are not where I am. We collide in a critical intimacy where what I say is only possible because it has been made so by things that they've already said. A method for living, of sorts, this intimacy is rugged. This intimacy fissures boundaries imposed, a method that methodically interrogates methodology. Methodological interrogation is the fugitivity I will be speaking about; it is a way of inhabiting the world, a posture of interrogation and refusal, like on some perpetual *Nah*-type shit; a breaking of the regime that tried to fix us but didn't know that we arose in the breaking, were made by a breakage that generates the refusal to be broken. A sustenance by way of getting out of the maelstrom of the typical is what I mean. The sustenance is engendered by experimentation, improvisation, unruliness, because their rules stifle what comes in the break of the cut. It's where we keep finding life lived otherwise, life on the run in inexhaustible exhaustion.

If this running is a political, disruptive act, then here I want to engage that disruption, revel in it, let it flex on 'em with humbled hubris. The life of my mind, my intimate, my private past, is, as any feminist worth their salt will tell you, deeply political. I want to speak from that private, underground place where sinners dwell, where sin as a transgressive act against divine law is what is shared between us; where we keep open secrets of queer conspiracies whispered on underground rooftops; where we use vernacular, words that break free of grammar's lexical dictates: we *fix* food instead of cook it, *cut* instead of turn lights on, so they can't figure out what we talmbout. Our den of sin, as it were, our promiscuous and shadowy presence, preserves a space for stowaways to be, and choose to be, stowed. This is fugitive coalition, fugitive kinship. This shadowy, stowaway presence, reminiscent of wrecked ships—which is to say, ships we have brought wreck to—is the knowledge and livelihood of fugitivity.

I grew up in Philly and its outskirts, where hip-hop was our unofficial language (Power 99 FM; 100.3 The Beat!), unlaced Timberland boots and Carhartt jackets were our unofficial uniforms, summer mornings were the color of orange juice mixed with fresh blood, and you carried an entire archive of meaning based on which part of Philly you repped. We lived right next to an abandoned house, no porch—like, that shit was just gone—so my cousin Marcus and I would go down into the basement of the house, rummaging around in the subterranean belly of its structure, before we'd get scared and run out. (Well, *I* got scared.) Unbounded curiosity, we youngbuhls had. To dare to explore without the presumption of conquest, an exploration of the interstices of the indoors with the wilderness-knowledge of the outdoors, is an outlawish and out-of-lawish praxis. And it stretched to our imaginations: we revised video game narratives, yearning for larger worlds. We imagined worlds filled with live Pokémon, with Charizard's and Mewtwo's tenacity. We lived loudly in our minds, oozing with vitality while simultaneously surrounded by poverty. We tried to remain afloat, but some of us did not, as they misguidedly say, "make it." Marcus fell prey to the conditions that middle-fingered our lives from our inception. His thin 6'3" frame not eradicated, but reduced to being bound indoors with cigarettes and television. Now, more than two decades later, still two years older than me, still funny on the sneak, still with calligraphic handwriting, Marcus rests largely skill-less and jobless after a raucous bout with drugs—marijuana, cocaine, heroin too—and diagnosed schizophrenia. What happened here, cuz? What stingy alchemy concocted a brew so pungent as to singe your flourishing?

He seemed to have picked up a fate similar to that of so many people we cohabited around. The plight of the Black and poor. But I am awed, truly, at how joyous and dope our lives were despite the fact that we were geographically destined for not only economic but also emotional poverty. I am awed, in other words, at how we still live. We crack jokes in the face of abjection. Like that Christian messiah who did not die, who is said to live perpetually in the all of the world, we have always and already risen, Jesus-like, because the only ones who can feed that many people with such paltry rations are "big mamas." It's like Double Dutch in the streets, making the passing cars wait until you trip up—*but you never trip*; like laughing at cartoons, your body and the TV on the floor so the bullets flying inches above you from drive-bys don't interrupt Spongebob and Patrick's shenanigans; like cookouts where your niece is telling everyone how beautiful her dark skin is because the sun loved her so, so, soooo much, or where your uncle is acting a fool, talking about how he "still got it" even after his six decades of life. *Despite every reason not to, we still smile, we still laugh, we still love, we still Black, y'all. We still.*[1] We lived, we sang, we danced, we gleaned textured life from a milieu that said we weren't supposed to celebrate our own existence. Our joy was, and still is, radical.

We made do with what we did and didn't have. Imaginative games became not only fun but also life-sustaining. We flourished in the face of abjection, like *Nah, we don't do that over here.* And we made do, in the simplest of ways. Like, you wanna play some basketball? Well, you ain't got no court, but you do have a milk crate, some nails, and a telephone pole. We cut out the bottom of one of those orange milk crates, climbed on somebody's shoulders, hammered some nails into that jawn, and voilà, basketball in the 'hood. I was forged in this resilient and inventive space.

But when I wasn't shooting hoops—or rather, shooting crates—I dwelled in the recesses of my own fraught mind, the "break" in which Black life is situated, where unavoidable subjection meets a radical breakdown. Or a radical boogeydown. I was a precocious kid, but quiet. I preferred to listen—listen for knowledge, for language, for the texture of the in-between space housing the incendiary edges of life. I'd lay low, though that is not to say that something wasn't going on. I spoke infrequently, as I understood the consequences of speaking out of turn, "talking back." In the "old school" from which Mom and Grandma hail, where they plait switches to tear into insolent young-sters, children were meant to be seen, not heard; they were meant to be obedient, to stay in line, which stifled my unchained and unchain-able thoughts. But I knew not to invite punishment, the backhand lick, the slap across the face that would catch you off guard, the *I wish you would.* My laying-low covert ops were a strategy of survival, a way to ensure the continuation of the thoughts they couldn't stop me from thinking.

My brother Gordon was, in a word, troublesome. (Though he, my sister, and I all have different fathers, there was never a sense of

us being "half" siblings. There was nothing "half" about our relationship, so I ask you, reader, to accord our siblingship the fullness
you'd accord others.) Three and a half years my senior, he made the
world his playground, a sandbox full of possibility, swings of pen-
dulous danger and ebullience, and a slide racing toward a perpetual
laugh amid strife, LOLing even in a cauldron of uncertainty. Gordon
was the one out wreaking havoc, cuttin' up in the streets, operating
in the existential space between criminality and revolution: always
on the move and, ever since his youth, never sitting still (despite the
prescribed Ritalin's attempt to rein him in to docility), because that's
how fugitives live—on the move. He trained, indirectly, Marcus and
me. We followed his lead, his humor, his love of life's levity. Whether
we were teamed up playing video games, trying to practice our skills
on the ball court to be like him, or creating imaginative games to
assuage the "Yo, I'm *bored*," we wanted to achieve his cool, that affect
of troublesomeness and noncompliance.

But me, I mean, I was a real homebody as a kid. I liked the house.
It was safe, knowable. I'm not one, and my mother would agree, to rip
and run in the streets. Not really "grassroots," the meaning of which
I'm still not entirely sure of. I was never—and am still not—one to go
out and march in the streets, protesting The Man. But y'all go 'head,
because The Man needs a good talking to, and maybe one of Grandma's switches. I, though, prefer to dwell in thoughts, in ideas, where
I can do the work I do. I inherit a tradition that has etched itself into
existence through sheer will, gainsaying opposition because it had no
choice, penning fire on pages that stretch across geographies and tem-
poralities. I dwell in the volatility of the outdoors even while within
the walls of the home. Writing and using language, that is what I do,
because in these acts radicality has ample room to huff and puff and
blow this place down. I raise my fist, hold my banner, chant my outrage
in fresh ink on the page. When I am withdrawn in my mind, marching
to a cogitative beat, I am putting in work. This is my lane, and others

have theirs; we do different types of labor all in the service of putting in the work necessary to bring the regimes of this world to an end.

This is all to say that we continue to escape confinement. When met with circumscription, we move because we kneel at the altar of swiftness. Those of us who have been cruelly disposed of, and those of us who understand disposedness as an ethical site of critical interrogation of that which created the conditions of disposedness, will not stand still. Being accosted by the violence of the normative—the imposition of an intransgressible, illimitable, unconsented-to order—responds to that fracturous escape that has in fact preceded us, a fracturous escape that we must choose to claim, continually, all of us. In doing that, we come together as fugitives in unruly harmony.

My grandmother is a philosopher. I mean that quite literally. When she reclines in her La-Z-Boy, arthritic knees elevated, gazing at her 55″ TV, she is thinking thoughts that do not look like thoughts. I've had hour-long seminars with my grandmother, her reclining and me lounging on the couch next to her, watching something thoroughly trite. And class begins. *He so stupid!* she says, at someone's idiocy. *Shouldn't've even been in there in the first place. He shoulda took his behind back home.* I always wonder, and sometimes ask, "Why he so stupid, Grandma?" and get little more than "'Cause he is." To most, this is less than fruitful. But she always makes me wonder what else is going on, what more is churning. There is always more to my grandmother. Something I can only imagine as the professorial musings of a savant is going on.

When she confides in me about the time she spends, after my mother has already left for work, getting my sister ready for school in the morning—ensuring she gets dressed, eats breakfast, forgets nothing—or having dinner ready for her after school; fielding requests from other children about whether TT can come outside; monitoring my sister's attitude and TV time; or even keeping mental track of how much money, down to the cent, is "on [her] Mac card," she is going on in low-key lecture style about the distribution of domestic labor. She engages the lineage of Selma James, Claudia Jones; she does it better than Marx.

When she cautions me about taking SEPTA, Philly's public transit, she is drawing on a rigorous sociological analysis of the landscape. *They crazy out there* is backed up by an archive so vast as to make my bibliographic citations seem paltry. Her knowledge is a cloak of survivalistic foresight. Who needs Kevlar when Grandma has already delivered instructions to evade any ills I might encounter? Who needs to reinvent the artful dodge when she already turned us over to the world shrouded in elusive edification?

When she catches somebody in a lie she won't say that they're lying; rather, she'll say they're "telling stories." The use of "telling stories" instead of "telling lies" was so pervasive growing up, and the very word *lying* connoted so negatively, I could have sworn that *lying* was a bad word. I thought, forreal-forreal, that it was functionally equivalent to saying *shit*. But alas, telling stories, what poet Kevin Young has called "storying," is a dexterous linguistic maneuver that tethers Black radical traditions together via invention. Its lineage is robust. Grandma was dropping knowledge on me and I didn't even know it. How adept of her. Her arthritis ain't touched her linguistic skills.

My mother, Grandma's only daughter, on the other side of the same hand, is polyphonic. She is more than herself. From her exudes the eloquent cacophony of those who have fashioned her epic stature and her imposing attitudinal heft (and I mean *attitude* in the most commendatory of ways). Her wisdom is a polyphonic many-voicedness, consolidating the knowledge of the multitude of Black women who have enabled her, unmerged, coexisting rapturously. Riotous laughter, shade-throwing witticisms, and incisive bullshit detection from decades of navigating ain't-shit men and people who think they slick are the "historical and concrete plenitude of actual social-historical languages" that Mom enacts with polyphonic fidelity.[2]

I recall a moment in my youth, perhaps a moment that many young boys who cried too much like me have experienced, when my mother sat me on her lap and told me, soothingly yet at the same time expressing pain, that I needed to be a big boy. I was a crybaby up until an age that was too old by most standards, my brother always chiding me for "crying for no reason," my mother sometimes threatening to "really give you something to cry about." But my mother, at least in this pithy moment, calmed me into big-boyness, a lesson she inherited somehow, from somewhere, one that held weight and novelty. My crying immobilized me, so her soothing was meant to usher in a refusal of rigidity in me. My mother's soothing, her polyphonic setting-in-motion, was an enablement of fugitive escape from lachrymose stillness.

Too, Mom was devoted to the well-being of her children. She looked out for hers in a way that, at times muted and at times simmering and still other times stentorian, ensured the proliferative *jouissance*—in a Black motherworking appropriation of French philosophy—of burgeoning Black life. Karate lessons? Done. Boy Scouts? Bet. Basketball practice? Cool. This is a long history of magic-making, an art handed down by generations of craftswomen, my mother hearing and speaking the voices in a kind of genealogical glossolalia. The magic is neither fantastic nor otherworldly; it is a magic that escapes our ability to pin it down in words. It is a fugitivity that evades our ability to grasp it because, ever the elusive concept, its unspeakability is characteristic of its origins in a tradition of those who built their life on critiquing the existing terrain, demanding not merely more space, inclusion even less; no, this magic demands a refusal of the very tenets of what exists.

And more, Mom carried authority—a side-to-side-and-back kind of authority rather than top-down—that seeped into her from a myriad of places, from folks I've never met and some she's never met either, but folks who are kin to us, folks who made sure we could live.

A polyphonic authority, my mother's verbal authorship of commands fundamentally alters the terrain, making authority "no longer [able to] monopolise the 'power to mean'" because her *'Cause I said so* exceeds her and exists before her.[3] She said so, just 'cause, because Grandma said so, her mother said so, Auntie and cousin said so. "'Cause I said so" exists in excessive multiplicity in my mother, given weight by a lineage that has seen some things. Her "I" is more than her. Her "I" does not agree to the rules of singular subjectivity contained by presumptions of individualist authority. This polyphonic life my mother fashioned in our home is a refusal, a refusal of the ways in which the world imposes singular sovereignty on our lives. We can only mean one thing, the world tells us, so my mother's latching of an entire world to her utterances is an ardent rebuff of the gestures of individuality. When she speaks, she does so with a legion of others who come back, though they never left, showing us that we live together.

These are the people who set the fugitive seed in my intellectual soil and gave me the chance to grow, the people who, in Dickensian parlance, raised me by hand. They have sent me to engage my gifts, so I am acquiescing: writing it down, letting them speak through me, because this story is not only mine. It is so much theirs too, as is any story I tell, any knowledge I claim to have. I'm here because something and someone else made it possible for me to be here. I am nothing more or less than, but something indistinguishably more and less than, the excavated relics from the sand that others before me have done the labor of working out. I am the refuse of splendid work that started long ago, a splendidness that peeks through the apertures of the ways in which I heed the lineages moving me to speak. I, like you, am entangled.

What I've extracted from the fugitive debris in which I was reared, a fugitivity inflected by that demanding nexus of Black and woman, is that it names a way of living together in the undercurrents of governance. It is not necessarily a model or template; it is, in fact, defiant of these. It is a flash, a glimmer, a flicker that forces us to see and do differently. It engenders our doing something, not our being something; it engenders our moving with others on unruly grounds.

These are the people, the "from," that oldheads always urge me to "never forget." I may have left Philly and those concrete slabs from which roses grow, but my exit is not a pathological flight; it is a dispersal that refuses denial, a feast on the move, still imbibing and devouring that Black vernacular and that ghetto twang that nourish me. It is an embrace of the generative disorder that causes the dissonance of staying there but living somewhere else. I will never forget the people and places from which I come, because I cannot; indeed, they sent me away to do my work, a sending away that has brought them too. So perhaps I can offer more than a glimpse and show just how real it can get when we listen to the stentorian voices of the marginalized; the undiscovered songbirds; the illest artists you'll never know; the slain dark-skinned angels; and the unadulterated faces of something like divinity in the ghettos, prison cells, preschools, projects, plantations, and slave ships.

Here in these pages, I want to show that I, too, sing America, but with a raspy, shitty, rough vocal timbre that might not sound like singing. I want to map out the thoughts I have circling around my mind in hopes that someone will feel me in haptic intimacy. Right here in these pages—*this shit right here . . .*—I also want to "sit with Shakespeare," along with Du Bois who penned those words in 1903; I want to "move arm in arm with Balzac and Dumas."[4] But instead of French writers, I want to move arm in arm with the misfits, the deviants, the lowlifes and imbeciles, the poor and the uneducated, because rebellious knowledge happens underground.

Them Goon Rules

Tell the coppers "hahahaha" you can't catch 'em, you can't
stop 'em
I go by them goon rules, if you can't beat 'em, then you
pop 'em.

— Lil Wayne, "A Milli"

Know that when I say I yearn for a criminal side hustle, I mean no harm, only other ways to be that are, in the current state of things, illegal. Know that what they've given us is insufficient because, though it tries desperately, it cannot contain our breadth. Where we spill over is marked as undesirable, against the law, wrong, nonexistent. But they don't know. They can't, 'cause it's outside their grasp, causing them to denigrate it by corralling it into their folds. But we don't like their rules, can't abide by them, can't live within them. What we have is different.

Though I am decidedly no fanboy of Lil Wayne, the dude said something really insightful in his 2008 smash hit "A Milli." That jawn—and *jawn* is like a mathematical variable, an X that can stand in for any noun, according to the logic of Philly slang—was blasting from the cars of everybody on my block, had all the guys on my football team like "a milli, a milli, a milli, a milli, a mill, a mill, a milli, a milli, a milli. . . ." Maddening, really. But Wayne rhymed a perceptive two bars in the first verse: "Tell the coppers 'hahaha' you can't catch 'em, you can't stop 'em / I go by them goon rules, if you can't beat 'em, then you pop 'em." Wayne is on to something really penetrative here, a kind of Blackness I'd say, a fugitive Blackness.

What I mean by *fugitive* is having a sensibility for outlawry. But not like a Wild West bandit shootin' up saloons and riding off on horseback in an upkick of dust. A fugitive, and fugitivity, references stolen life. Fugitivity marks a kind of outlawish indiscreet disavowal of and disengagement from the project of hegemony. Hegemony is the culprit, or more specifically normativity is, a normativity understood as a pervasive manner of forcing a fundamental, impenetrably bounded beingness through an oppressive and nonconsensual violation. This normativity posits itself as impossible, and unlawful, to be gotten outside of. It stultifies one's ability to exceed captivity. The fugitive's relation to being captured, a capture that is a subjection to an unbreachable law, is reducible neither to avoidance nor simple inversion: it is a refusal, a primary nonconsent. It is in the motion of the unthought and appositional, the underside-underground and edginess of order, that fugitivity gains its heft. Fugitives are ruled by unruliness, which is no rule at all, but rather a *movement* in which life is garnered, in which the improper thrives due to its obstinacy. Refusing to sit still, refusing to settle, refusing to commit to being is the fugitive's lot.

Or, to use Lil Wayne's words, the fugitive, in the face of the "coppers"— a proxy for all that attempts to violently capture or exterminate—says "hahahaha." A hearty laugh that signifies both playfulness and mischievousness. Informative of this is the trajectory in which exposures of holes in the State's powers highlight their ultimate illegitimacy. The structures that bind try so hard to quell insurgency because of structure's constant teetering relation to obsolescence. Its rules can always be broken. Indeed, those rules do not apply; those rules do not and cannot rule. Hence, to "go by them goon rules" is a praxis of unruliness in the sense that the deviancy cast upon those who undermine systemic rule is mobilized in service of the deviant. This unruliness, this lawlessness— which is not, mind you, a bacchanalian war zone of licentiousness—is the start of an ethical sociality. If the Law is a normative regime that rests on a fundamental violence, it stands that the subversion of Law precipitates the beginning of a nonviolent way of relating to one another. Where we've engendered trouble is where the violence is broken down. Goon rules propel trouble, or bear the mark of that which brings trouble. And the trouble that is a goon's refusal to kowtow to the Law is not inactivity or an absence of a plan that stalls "real change." Goon rules exist in the "undercommons": where debts are unpaid, the gates are left open, and the troubles of the world are not the object of our smooth ire but the worldly conditions that made our trouble possible. Followers of the (non)rules of the goons echo the underlying subversive lower frequencies; they make noise, revel in its cacophony, and refuse to structure it into something that others say sounds like music.

On Whiteness

> *Whiteness is not a kinship or a culture. White people are no more closely related to one another, genetically, than we are to black people. . . . What binds us is that we share a system of social advantages that can be traced back to the advent of slavery in the colonies that became the United States. . . . For me, whiteness is not an identity but a moral problem.*
>
> — Eula Biss, "White Debt"

A quick word on white folks: I love me some white people. My thoughts on Blackness are not meant to diss you, white folks, though neither am I here to put you at ease (be assured: I am not). My beef is not with white people; it's with *whiteness*. My problem is with the extent to which those of you who are said to be white—and even those of us who aspire to get cozy with whiteness—are seduced by the allure of whiteness. Whiteness is a kind of ideology, a violent way of inhabiting oneself racially,

and it is whiteness that operates pervasively as one of dominative power's ligaments. It naturalizes itself and becomes "lifestyled," simply the
way of the world; trying to change that would be to dare to alter the
natural order of things. Whiteness, in other words, be drawlin.'
Whiteness marks itself as pure and unmarred while marking Blackness, for example, as in need of reform (read: assimilation, annihila-
tion). Whiteness "invisibilizes" the labor of the nonwhite and thinks
that the immense wealth the nation has acquired was due solely to its
gumption and greatness. It's because whiteness is fragile, so timid and
so easily threatened by being called out. Like, a white woman, who had
just learned that I studied Black feminism and Black studies, asked,
"So you think about white supremacy?" to which I responded, simply,
"I do, yes, and many, many more things." She responded immediately:
"Well, I don't think I'm better than any other race, I love all kinds of
people." ". . . Okay?" was all I could muster. "Just saying," she said. Yes,
yes you are just saying.

A whiteness that feels so threatened by references to the white
supremacist legacy of the country or to whiteness's detrimental and
fatal effect on bodies of Color crafts new stories of identity, stories
that depict itself as patriotic, unmarred by bias, self-sufficient, Christian and godlike, and the sole cultural force that founded this country. Because these people feel so threatened by having their space of
normativity challenged, they retrench themselves in false histories of
their own—and this country's—racial purity and purported individual not-thinking-they're-better-than-any-other-race.

And it can afflict anyone. We are all of us susceptible to its allure,
as it, in James Baldwin's terms, is not racial identity per se but a met-
aphor for power. Power entices all of us and beckons for us to agree
with its reality, a reality to the detriment of those who refuse power's
oppression, power's malice, power's normativity. Because those who
adhere to whiteness can't be reliably and systematically peeped by
recourse to the visual, we need to maintain a critical stance and rally

around those who, like us on that goon rules tip, fugitively refuse power's grasp. Our fellow goons can be a range of hues. And so can those who are trying to have us killed.

There is a way in which the narrative of the country, perhaps of the world, traffics in imagined conversations with fabricated ghosts. These conversations skew toward the nonsensical and contradictory. Adamant barking about historical equality, contemporary equity, and future utopias is uttered amid the tumult of their inverse. What is shouted is not the case. Cries about the mattering of the depths of character unwittingly defy the impossibility of this. We yearn for a transparency that we must in fact evade. These are dreams that founded this sense of national superiority. Stubborn dreams in which we sip tea—pinky extended, keepin' it classy—with phantoms that never existed. We are indeed a nation of dreamers, wishing not to awaken from nocturnal fantasies. But in this is grave danger. My man Mos Def has already told you: "Evacuate your sleep, it's dangerous to dream."[1]

One, two, Freddy's coming for you . . . .

Blackness and Fugitivity*

"Blackness" as an alternative ethics of the sacred, a practice of primordial commoning in excess of (racial) capitalism. So understood, blackness is not, strictly speaking, just another identity. Being for all people, blackness bespeaks intimacy without limit, belonging without borders, care and caress without rule/s. The sacred otherwise.

— J. Kameron Carter

---

*Parts of this section were originally published on *The Coffeelicious* under the title "I Like My Coffee Black: Fugitive Blackness (With Gratitude to Fred Moten)," on May 25, 2016.

The subversive force of goon rules manifests an understanding of a kind of Blackness. I've caught some flak for my thinking with respect to Blackness, for affixing Blackness to fugitivity, for making Nahum Chandler's "paraontological distinction"—a super-fancy way of saying what Zora Neale Hurston has said: "All my skinfolk ain't kinfolk." From head-shaking disapproval to the flippant foreclosure of further discussion, I've encountered a surfeit of disbelief, shock, and accusations of abstract disconnect from lived experience. What often goes unheard, at the very least, is my yearning for something else to be, for a coalition with all those weird and radical folks based on an identity found in our intimacy. Can we shake foundations, categories, history, but not get shook? This is no argument that primarily seeks to convince and persuade; this is an insistent wandering, wondering about something that might enable unruled livability and ungoverned life. You see, I want *the otherwise*, an otherwise that's in excessive refusal of what we have now and holds the possibility—the open, radical, tortuously scary possibility—of thinking Blackness as proximal primarily to fugitivity and fugitivity as a desirable side hustle that inaugurates us all, to the extent that we hustle hard, into Blackness. I want it, that is, to be the illegibly glossolalic subtlety, with monstrous consequences, engendered in refusal to recite our catechisms, our shoulders a doubled Luciferian perch.

It seems that some do not think I "get it," that I simply don't understand that to *be* Black rests on an optics and experiential reality, nothing much more. They think I don't know. I want to laugh—"'hahahaha' you can't catch 'em. . . ."—because y'all must've forgot. I have come to know precisely what you all attest to, on an intimate level: at the level of ontology, the all-up-in-and-on-me of vitriol lashed at me solely on the grounds of what they perceive to be a kind of criminality or inferiority exuding from my epidermis. I am only suspicious of it all and want to proliferate interest in the "subterranean alien/nation of black things in their unregulatable chromaticism."[2] See, I just want to, ever so apprehensively, deregulate the affixation of Blackness to chromatics and place it elsewhere, in the critical intimacy we share with one another when we come together to pull things apart. Believe me, I know very well all the quippy retorts. It's difficult to naïvely posit that I don't get it when I can tell you some stories. . . .

I.

So I'm minding my own business, as I'm wont to do, and a young white woman I've known only a handful of days says to me, "You should *fix* your hair, you *need* to pick it out."

"No I don't," I respond to her. "It's perfectly fine." She shakes her head, as if I'm a toddler cringing at the prospect of broccoli for dinner.

Now, this for sure is no new phenomenon—white folks have long been policing and disciplining the hair of Black folks and other folks of Color. It is a means by which hair, as a site of demanded professionalism, is coerced to assimilate, to straighten up, to be presentable. In alignment, that is, with whiteness. Refusal of the assimilationist sentiment means one must be a bit mad. But what is a madman, and other madpeople, to do when accosted with the tumultuous blight of demanded respectability—or else? This is the delirious dilemma of one who is said to be, and who is in danger of becoming, mad. *Surely* my hair needs fixing and straightening. One would be mad to think otherwise. But declarations of madness invoke the fragility of power; power expresses its tenuousness, its fearful, fearful flimsiness.

From the time I was a child, I suffered through my mother's heavy-handedness, a heavy-handedness that she too would confirm. Though she will not apologize for it. My brother and I, when cornrows were still a thing that didn't get you clowned, would sit between my mother's knees, that blue-green grease on the back of her hand for efficient access, while she tugged on our hair with no regard for the incipient tears welling in my eyes. I'm telling you, that shit hurt (or *hurted*, as we pronounced it back then). Over a year we endured that twice-monthly ritual, often more frequent for me since I took up the habit of unsuturing a few rows while I was at school because they were too tight, too constricting. I just could not abide the taming.

Eventually I asked my mom to give me locs; she obliged, and the more infrequent management was welcome. They grew gradually, but soon my brother's friends and kids at school started teasing me for them, my hair's joyous scatter the subject of ridicule. I wanted out after nine months with them. And for years after, it was trips to the barbershop every two weeks.

But I've since reflected on the turmoil my hair has caused in its various forms, and it all, to me, points to a pervasive unwillingness to incorporate the unruliness my hair signified. From the taming commentary by white women to the taming hands of my mother to the taming rhetoric of middle-school children to the taming blades of Wahl clippers, all were various iterations of an aesthetic normativity that was unhappy with my hair's breach of decorum. It wasn't until college that I, literally, said, "Fuck it," and let my hair do its own thing. How cruel, I thought, to have never allowed it to grow, that literal blackness rising incrementally from my head, peering out into the world. Ever since, my hair and I, in a crooked and oppositional sense of the standard definition, or in the recalibrated definitional sense of the vernacular: we straight.

My hair and its unruliness bespeak a small rebellion that is ever ongoing. It is an always-on gesture toward not being hedged, quite literally, and this is a manifestation—among many, many others of varying sizes—of fugitivity, of perhaps follicular goon rules. We rocked fros back in the '70s when we raised our fists in defiance, so this is a lineage in which I, too, engage. This is why they, sometimes, get scared: because my and others' illustrious naps, a phrasing construed as oxymoronic and paradoxical, evoke power's untenability.

What is this anxiety I spark? Insecurities abound, displaced onto the unruliness signified by the unkempt.

I'm hiding secrets & weapons in there. . . .[3]

II.

There exists a pervasive police presence. It is no accident that Lil Wayne's proxy for dominant power is the "coppers." It is a name, of many, that cites the spirit of surveillance and discipline. A name for the *top-flight security of the world, Craig.* It is at base a name for Law itself, and to laugh at its iterations is to laugh at, and undermine, the Law. And undermining the Law means you feel its wrath. And we feel this viscerally.

In fact, I actually got arrested once. *Gasp!* (Little ol' me? Unbelievable.) I was with a group of maybe twelve people, only half of whom I was actually friends with. We had been playing "Manhunt" at the park until we had eggs thrown at us. We walked home, half of us causing a ruckus, hitting stop signs, yelling. Disruptive teenage stuff, you might say. Me, as usual, quiet and chill as can be. Cops stroll by and give us a warning. Everybody's like, "Sorry, officers. We'll be quiet. We're just on our way home." Mind you, it was like 10:45 p.m. and curfew was 11 p.m. We go to the Wawa—think 7-Eleven, Turkey Hill, Sheetz, whatever your local convenience store chain is—and make our way back to Mike's house to chill when, literally (and I mean *literally*) ten steps from his house, that 5–0 *Woop! Woop!* blares and the cops are like, "Okay, you had your warning, so now everyone get in." Mike, his brother, and his cousin get off the hook because Mike's mom comes out and vouches for them. (When social wealth bubbles up in the nick of time.) The rest of us, segregated by perceived gender, are told to file into the back of the paddy wagon.

The entire five-minute ride to the station, I said nothing. Too many stories running through my mind, the stories of those whose names you can probably begin to tally by sheer fatal memory at this point. We were told to sit on the floor when we were led into the station, everyone freaking out, the four young women with us crying. One kid asked to use my cell phone to call his mom. I then called my mom: "Mom, can you come pick me up from the Collingdale police station? I'll explain when you get here." Cool as a frozen cucumber, yo. But get this, and I lie to you not: while everybody else was hyperventilating, crying, or spazzing out in some form, I *giggled* to myself. One part shock at the surrealism of the whole situation, but one bigger part disavowal of the severity of the enforcement of law. One officer strutted and postured his power, stood in a way that enacted the law he sought to carry out. My giggles were not having that. Your "authority" is, quite literally, laughable.

Mom came with her boyfriend Rodney; I got in the car, told them what happened, and, because they know me, it was all good. "Now, if this was your brother, it'd be a different story," my mom said, Rodney concurring, only half-jokingly. I never told them about the laughing, though. But based on their reaction, I imagine they would have giggled right alongside me.

There is no "moral" to this story, only the deviously salvific laughter. It is a laugh of mischief. What is perhaps so enticing about the laugh, the muted giggle, is its sonic uncapturability. They cannot subject its sound to existent apparatuses of arrest. This sound—"hahahaha"—is a differentiation dispersed within all the noise in the surround. That differentiation is too elusive to be tied to normative regimes of meaning, so we find uncomfortable comfort in it, us goons. It defies for a moment the discreetness that allows for disciplinary policing. "Policing" is the act of subjecting to laws. These laws constrict my capacity to live. But by giggling, in some minuscule but substantive way, so small as to characterize an eclipse, I stole life back.

III.

I realize I'm saying some things that you think can get me in
trouble, but . . . I was born in trouble.

— Malcolm X, "At the Audubon"

I may here, if I haven't already, begin to say some things that might
propel me into a troublesome space. I might, again, because I was
reared and bred this way, become a problem by doing the work of
problematizing. But, as Malcolm X says in the epigraph above, I — to
be clear, and nowhere near twisted, *because of my Blackness* — was
born in trouble. Indeed, one might say that this is, at least in part, what
Blackness is, what Blackness means and signifies, does and portends:
trouble.

I met with a prospective English PhD student the day before he and
others in his potential cohort were to be shuttled through meetings,
meet-and-greets, lectures, and the academic like in an attempt to get
them to matriculate into our institution. A biracial dude studying hip-
hop, literature, and short stories, he was a dope scholar of theories of
miscegenation, which caused us to end up spending, like, five hours
chilling, talking, and vibing in Starbucks. And we didn't buy an ounce
of coffee.

As this student and I spoke, we wandered, inevitably as rigorous
thinkers of Black studies and general iconoclastic intellectual shit are
wont to do, onto the subject of the effects of Blackness.

"Blackness, if we think about what people like Ta-Nehisi Coates
or Claudia Rankine are getting at, is, I wanna say, something that is
not simply about this right here," he said as he vigorously rubbed his
caramel skin.

"Yes!" I said with a jolt, banging the table. And my response, perhaps, is a controversial point, but I mean it: "Blackness is deployable,
which is to say it is a fugitive, disruptive, iconoclastic, pathogenic

force perturbing normativity, normative whiteness." (I was in not-so-rare academic form that day.) Blackness has a kind of innate capacity to challenge power's normativity wherever it may emerge. In between criminality and propriety lies Blackness, that quotidian practice of refusal, the middle finger to reconciliation, decorousness, and the demand to structure its raspy vocal timbre into something, anything, that sounds like verified music.

Enter whiteness.

As we engaged in Black sociality in this public space—a no-no if there ever was one, a veritable insurgence beckoning, purportedly, to be policed, because when Blacknesses conspire together, ain't no way they talkin' 'bout anything other than how to get mo' free—this old white dude inserted himself into our conversation. No warning. No request. Just entered, because, apparently, this space was his.

"I think you two gentlemen would find this very interesting." He placed on the table a newspaper clipping and pointed at its title: "Cornell Republicans to Host Fox News Correspondent Kimberly Guilfoyle."

"That's not the word I would use to describe this," I said to him as I read the title. He didn't hear me, though I was nothing short of clear and assertive.

"I think it would be fun for you guys to think about," he said, again hearing nothing.

"That's *certainly* not the word I would use. Please go away now." Nothing. He kept talking, waxing oh-so-objectively about the good-ness, fairness, and balance this speaker would bring to the commu-nity. "Yo, go away now, please. We are done with you." I am telling you, reader, this dude quite literally was unable to acknowledge my agential presence in this moment, the will I so clearly expressed—that he go away. And I was irate. *No, no, no, I really didn't see you.*[4]

So if we are using my experience in Starbucks as a case study that signifies a pervasive phenomenon, we must ask ourselves what hap-

pens when Blackness occupies space codified through and by whiteness, so much so that embodied incarnations of this whiteness—a
whiteness, we must note, that was consolidated into its current inim-
ical identity through violence—are summoned to shut this Blackness
down. What happens when, in public, normative space, Blackness
comes NY-bopping in with the leg limpin', refuses the coffee of Starbucks, and rather prefers to be sippin' on sin and juice? Blackness
becomes the disposition, the posture, the moving force of *fugitivity*.

I am eternally indebted to Fred Moten for his recalibration of Blackness. We might say that this "thing" we call Blackness is the irreparable
disturbance of how stasis gets congealed. An ensemble and a revolutionary signifier of fissure, Blackness refuses to even acknowledge the
tenets of power. It refuses, gets bored with (*yaaawn*) authority that
attempts to circumscribe this disruptiveness. It is a sinister grin undermining prohibition because it possesses, and *re*possesses, knowledge
of the indecorous, the inappropriate.

Moten and his beloved comrade Stefano Harney help us more.
They write, pontificating-in-Black:

> The anoriginary drive and the insistences it calls into being and moves
> through, that criminality that brings the law online, the runaway anar-
> chic ground of unpayable debt and untold wealth, the fugal, internal
> world theater that shows up for a minute serially—poor but extrava-
> gant as opposed to frugal—is blackness which must be understood
> in its ontological difference from black people who are, nevertheless,
> (under)privileged insofar as they are given (to) an understanding of it.[5]

I would encourage you to read that again; it's better the second time,
trust me.

And then read it a third time.

Blackness, then, is lawlessness, a predisposition to break the Law
(note the capital) precisely because the Law is a violent force seeking

to preserve order. But to those of you who say, "We *need* laws and orderliness," it must be noted that the Law is distinct from *justice*. The Law, historically, has sanctioned—and still does, my god!—the obliteration of Blackness. Trans-Atlantic slave trade: Lawful. Black bodies as accumulated and fungible mere extensions of another *real* five-fifths human being: Lawful. Black codes: Lawful. Redemption: Lawful. Jim Crow, Jane Crow, and lynching: Lawful. The post–Thirteenth Amendment enslavement of "convicts": Lawful. Racially specific hyperincarceration: Lawful. Extralegal and vigilante extermination of Black insurgency via ground-standing and the exoneration of the murderous culprits: Lawful.

Again, "Law" is distinct from justice.

This anoriginary drive, which is to say a mutinous force that precedes its epidermal genesis, describes Blackness here. It is a pervasive breaking of the Law that comes before the Law and, because of the Law's violence, is in fact a criminality recalibrated as analgesic. This kind of criminality, because it responds to violence, is in fact an ethical alleviation of violence. A Blackness-as-fugitivity is a giddy-up, ante-up flighty movement. Reminiscent of the outlawry of marauding mavericks, the primordial giddy-up signals Blackness as outside Law, escapeful (because that marauder always escapes into the night, fleeing in, and perhaps through and because of, the darkness and blackness of the midnight hours); Blackness goes and goes, zooming in the heat of the night, enabled by, well, its Blackness. It's impure from the jump, an "interstitial drama on the outskirts of the order of purity," outskirts that skid outward toward an illegible edge, that arise with the *funk* of Blackness doing its work, sweating up a blustery flight from motionlessness, living life, its darkness telling tales.[6]

Runaway behavior, escape from the treacherous arms of structural power, might in fact save us. Where even on the flip side we don't get caught because we're in between the flip side and the side from which we got flipped. It is a kind of runaway spirit in which an untold charity is bestowed, time and again, inexhaustibly, because it is that which propels escape from capture; a life and liveliness on the lam, living in wilderness beyond policed and policing frontiers. And it wants all y'all. My skinfolk are "(under)privileged" in our understanding of this Blackness by way of history's mappings, the taxonomic "Blackness" of the epidermis an imposed proxy for that preexistent and insistent force of fugitivity.[7] But it is more than us (oh, how cliché this sounds, how old-fashioned), before and after us, and asks us to do fugitive work knowing that we can't pay back the debt of its wealth—a wealth that does not ask of us the taking of livelihood from others, rather a Satanic wealth that is inexhaustible, a wealth that is given, so long as we proliferate it, without having to exact the payment of anyone's life. This is wealth that we can all get in on if we choose to give it. And if we do that, we're kinfolk. "Blackness" names, gives discursive flesh to, a critical existence, a disobedient world-working, an irruption upon the norm that *crisisizes* the scene so we can reimagine the terms and meanings of the world in which we live.

To undermine the categorizing logic of the dominant through creative refusal. To disavow the governing attempts to adjudicate normative concoctions of difference. To forego coming together by way of some perceived genetic endowment in favor of a certain criminal, fugitive disposition. To clutch with open hands the insurgent imaginative flight. To take keen interest in the emblematizing of a pervasive and troubling irregularity that is open to all who desire, and do the work of enacting, the propelling force.

Blackness.

Let us then, please, think of Blackness as a radical movement of escape, as *stolen life*, as knowledge from the underbelly of the *Zong* and *Amistad*, where flesh melded languages, cultures, potentialities, and those dreams that are colder—and certainly more volatile—than death. Think of that elusive force that says uh-uh to being hedged by power. Let me be imperfectly clear here: Blackness is a kind of political category in substantive supplementation to that tied to epidermal identity. We move toward a textured and always incomplete inhabitation of Blackness, which is to say a disruptive posture toward the forces of hegemony. As Moten writes, "Choosing to be black implies *paying the cost*; it is a kind of *ethical* gesture to claim this dispossession, this nothingness, this radical poverty-in-spirit," or, in other words, as I so painstakingly try to refine and clarify: Blackness is trying to tarry in the fraught space between people deemed sufficiently epidermally Black and a fugitive, refusing spirit of escape.[8] That is, it's all good to think about the specificity of the social, material, and psychic phenomena that betide those who are read and interpreted as "Black," for this has historical import, but this also proves ultimately insufficient, necessitating, perhaps, thinking of Blackness, too, as the reworking and remixing of how we come to know and feel identity; as a mode of inhabiting the world predicated not on the physical surface but on a proclivity *to challenge and bring together all those deemed marginal and all those committed to liberatory politics.*[9] What is being called for in this advancement of a kind of Black queer radicalism is something super-difficult and, frankly, terrifying: to think of this thing very often affixed to viscerally felt physical difference as something in excess of that, as something sometimes, oftentimes, irrespective of that, as something that rests primarily on a subversive relation to power. That is, to think of one's nonnormative and oppositional relation to hegemony, and this primarily, as that which then allows one to understand oneself as/in Blackness, even as/in queerness and Black feminism. A radically subversive disposition, as it were, to fugitivity as such, which is to always index Blackness's "always already" queerness, its always already gender trouble. There is, then, an unbreakable relation between Blackness and its quint(non)essential definition of and as revolutionary politics.

I am not advocating Blackness as primarily a political identity that completely disregards the affective and historical, as well as material, purchase of epidermal classification, as if skin color is inconsequential. To be clear, I affirm one's feelings of finding community with skinfolk. This is a notable node of thinking with Blackness, yet not the only node, nor the node in which I am primarily interested. To belong with Blackness and in Blackness with others is not simply, or primarily, to end at the skin's surface; to belong with Blackness and in Blackness with others is more specifically a constantly contested commitment to a particular political posture. Blackness denotes a social dance-work skewing toward differentiation, one that is not possessed natally and *ad infinitum*. Blackness, y'all: *a particularly menacing angle perpendicular to everything*. Crooked spokes adjacent to what they've been told is their role in propelling the mechanic wheel.[10]

Put in profane vernacular reminiscent of the caustic speech used around the block: I'm not simply interested in fuckin' shit up; what I am genuinely interested in, on a different but related register, is the precise moment *when* particular actions or postures fuck shit up, and which things are fucked up, how they are fucked up, who fucks them up. Or more to the point, what is it about this thing deemed Black—what is its texture, its context, its history, its motivation for refusal; what is it 'bout—that foments the fuckin' up of that which is shit?

The Blackness I delineate here, to be frank and a bit controversial, is not concerned with authenticity or realness or "blood" or a possessed identity—though, sure, I guess it's kinda those things too. Blackness, as it is delineated here, is not concerned with itemizing a list of requirements that one must meet in order to—alas!—"be" Black, Jack. Nah, this Blackness ain't about that life.

Blackness, I assert, signifies that fugitive movement, absconding with life it is not supposed to have, refusing fixity. It speaks to that insurgent sociality that keeps on unfixing. Blackness dances in the underground, a dance that is itself a potent knowledge; it Crip Walks, Nae Naes (*watch me whip, whip!*), Lindy Hops, Dougies, and snaps its fingers in positional abjection but lived ebullience for the ungrammatizing, the anagrammatizing—the *in and out of place and time* pressure-putting *on meaning and that against which meaning is made*—of the norm.[11]

But all the while, it is constructively destructive, destructively constructive. It is what happens when Gizmo is satiated after midnight.

This is all to say that when Blackness is on unapologetic display in, say, a Starbucks, it may necessitate—to the extent that the space, like most spaces, is mired in the grammar of whiteness and anti-Blackness—that white dudes come and put their whiteness smack dab on display right in front of you, assuring you that it, whiteness, is "interesting" and "fun." Yes, they will try to come for you. But, as Blackness does, we will sidestep it, keep it movin', dance, sing, elude, escape, disrupt, and set fire to rain long before, and after, Adele. In short, Blackness will cause trouble, trouble, trouble.

The Dark Side

> *Can this being together in homelessness, this interplay of the refusal of what has been refused, this undercommon appositionality, be a place from which emerges neither self-consciousness nor knowledge of the other but an improvisation that proceeds from somewhere on the other side of an unasked question? Not simply to be among his [sic] own; but to be among his [sic] own in dispossession, to be among the ones who cannot own, the ones who have nothing and who, in having nothing, have everything. This is the sound of an unasked question.*
>
> —Fred Moten and Stefano Harney, *The Undercommons: Fugitive Planning & Black Study*

To traverse the dark side is to ask, unceasingly, the unasked question.

You see, I find immense value in wondering troublesome thoughts, in thinking those thoughts I ain't got no business thinking because they ain't got nothing to do with business thinking. Thoughts that misplace propriety, that displace legibility, that excavate the depths of our most radical modes of daring to think. This kind of thought, *insofar as it is genuine thinking, might best be conceived of as black thought*.[12] This kind of thinking that propels us into a kind of impossible escape from forces that attempt to capture us, which is to say fugitivity, y'all, is what it might mean to go by other rules—wildly other and othering rules. Goon rules. It seems that there is something immensely inviolable about a Blackness understood through fugitivity. The fact of Blackness's ability to flit from subject to subject, intersubjectively—and from subject *intra* subject, intrasubjectively— attests to its deployability. Blackness bespeaks less a sufficiency of melanin and more a way of thinking life and livability, a livability that posits itself in opposition and apposition to normative frameworks of life. To think Blackness in the vein of fugitivity serves as a synecdoche for those who enact a subjectivity on the dark side.

So in the spirit of "them goon rules," broken rules that ain't got no need to be fixed, fugitive rules that ain't got no time for rules, I want to propose that we trek on the dark side. The dark side becomes a habitual way of refusing the comforts of whiteness and the luxury of fittedness; the dark side, as a space one must choose to enter and remain inside, is a dwelling place that operates differently, so differently that it takes its toll on its inhabitants, makes them unruly, ornery, difficult, iconoclastic. It is fugitive space. When one moves on the dark side is when one enters into Blackness's fugitivity. Dwelling in and enacting one's subjectivity from the dark side is the deployment of the fissuring force that gives rise to nonnormativity's myriad inflections. By committing to the dark side, we engage a kind of fugitive subjectivity, which is characterized less by somatic endowment and more (much, much more) by commitment to living life in and from the darkness of the dark side.

Can we think about the dark side as a place that *makes* our identities through our intentional inhabitation of it? Can we be "dark-side people" who have a range of bodies and histories but, in our shared politicized darkness, are given to the world as a(n impossible) people? I care deeply about my kinfolk of the epidermal, gendered, embodied variety. Don't get that twisted. At the same time, too, I'm not sure my primary concern in garnering a community rests in whether we both got that melanin or if we both hail from the same block. What kind of work are you putting in, though? *That work.* Getting gully on and in the dark side is a testament to doing, a testament to how we make meaning and matter in the excess. That's my people, my kinfolk.

One of my dearest friends, Danny, has taught me much about kin. When his given family forsook him after he was vulnerable enough to live his sexual truth, he learned that family is not what one is tied to immutably by blood or chromosome, or even by salvific foster care and adoption (as Danny was adopted at age six). No, family is forged in the trenches with love, worked at and gotten to asymptotically since family is always incomplete, requiring a constant leap. Kinship begotten in the fugitivity of Blackness's coalitional drive cradles Danny's and my companionship, a "companionship that unsettles any arbitrary enclosures suggested by body, border, self, matter."[13] Danny and I are in the dark together, with a whole bunch of other folks who synesthetically see without light, our co-dwellers on the dark side who move, always, with furtive fugitive movements—movements of thought, movements of gait, movements of flesh, movements of subjectivity. We are, or are at least trying really hard at, moving beneath the normative gaze that structures proper thought and proper inhabitation of the world. We are we in here, regardless of who we be or who we were. Here, we can be we together, bumping into one another in critical intimacy, coming up with new ways to be, new ways to think. I like it in here, in the dark; all my people are here with me.

Danny has shown me the dark side in so many ways, a dark side that can finally accommodate the girth of our ties to each other. He showed me that we can live. Together. Familially. There are other ways, otherwise ways, to be familied. I am (un)bound familially to those people I live and fight and love with in the mythico-theological Underworld of different kinds of creaturely relations. If we dare to inhabit the work required of us on the dark side, thinking dangerously, our intellectual work runs from categorical legibility and reworks fugitive flight as the condition of collective togetherness. Danny is one of my goons, and I am one of his, going by different rules in the dark.

On Being Called a Thug

The worst words revivify themselves within us, vampirically. Injurious speech echoes relentlessly, years after the occasion of its utterance, in the mind of the one at whom it was aimed: the bad word, splinterlike, pierces to lodge. In its violently emotional materiality, the word is indeed made flesh and dwells amongst us—often long outstaying its welcome. Old word-scars embody a "knowing it by heart," as if phrases had been hurled like darts into that thickly pulsating organ, but their resonances are not amorous. Where amnesia would help us, we can't forget.

— Denise Riley, "Bad Words"

I walk down the small collegiate hub of my Ivy League graduate institution as it saturates quickly with backpack-clad students seeking food or sunlit reprieve or a place to study. I roam through space in cargo sweats, a tank top bookended by shoulders and arms with an increasing tattoo count, and a black bandanna. My visage is stern, scowling even, but only because I am thinking, as I'm wont to do. My phone vibrates.

It is April 2015, not a month before the Baltimore riots in which Black physicality will be put to work in the streets demanding to be seen, heard, recognized. In which time and again commentators and laypersons will castigate the rioters because they aren't being "peaceful" or quiet or docile. In which these same commentators will hijack

Dr. King's "nonviolent" philosophy, exalting docility for the weak and destructive cannons for the powerful. In which Toya Graham, the Baltimore "Mom of the Year," will beat her rioting son not, as she was falsely praised for, to reprimand him for doing the whole protest thing wrong, but because she didn't want her only son, her "everything," to become another Freddie Gray. Sounds like something my mom would do. How auspicious, then, that she and my mother have the same first name.

I peer at the text message from a woman whom I love and who has grown incredibly dear to me, an emoji of leering eyes indicating that one of her friends has spotted me. "Why are you spying on me?" I ask in jest. She responds: "Not me, somebody told me they saw you. She said you look like a thug." I reply: ". . . no comment." My frustration rests closely behind those two words. This not a month before media sources will swell with headlines branding rioters as "thugs" and the subsequent critiques, namely from Soledad O'Brien, averring that "'thug' is a proxy for 'N-word.'" I wonder: What's in a thug, those "hardcore [*cool record-scratching sound*] real ill niggas" that Rakim rhymes about? Text translation: "She said you look like a [big, scary goddamn nigger]."

I've been likened to a thug ever since I put on some muscle and got my first tattoos. Like race, the idea and image of a Thug (capital *T*) happens—indeed, thugs *happen*, they are a phenomenological occurrence—in the gap between appearance and the perception of difference, streamlined through a history that has emblematized criminality through a proximity to Blackness. My "being" a thug is about what people see and what they think they see, and what they think about when they see me. It's bigger than just my personal affinities, preferences, or tastes. To be called a thug, that word hurled at me and inevitably landing on, sticking to, my flesh, is to involuntarily harbor a calcified scab. My mind "angrily fondle[s] those names it had once been called"—"thug," "nigga," "jail-body," "gangsta"—reminding me, always, that "there's a habitual (if not inevitable) closeness between accusation and interpellation; there's also an echolalic, echoic aspect of interpellation itself," as Denise Riley says.[1] I am always at risk of thinking that *I am* the thug who could be justifiably murdered. The names I may be called shuffle dangerously close to making me call myself those names. And this danger lingers. I am hailed by a persecution that did not know me until I appeared on the scene—a persecution that in many ways is responsible for how I am *able* to appear on the scene—and once we meet, each instance of my appearance becomes populated by persecution's ghost, rendering me murmurously guilty on every occasion. Once I am called a thug, the name's force is so powerful as to coax me into repeating the sting in my mind over and over, long after the hostile word has been thrown. I cannot forget it; the anamnesis, the "unstoppable aural flashbacks," concatenate into a form of verbal PTSD, portending my murder.

Like Darren Wilson's description of Mike Brown, I exist in others' gazes as a demon. Demonic, yes, an insurgent incarnation of pure evil comin' to getcha getcha; too, though, a demon in a different sense, that figure of unpredictability and indeterminacy that lurks within a world presumed divine. I disturb the world's ability to fully tout its perfection, its imperialistic universal applicability. I am that question mark haphazardly—or ever so intentionally—filled in with inevitable criminality. With, in a word, thuggishness.

People arrive at my thuggishness not because of illegal or criminal activity on my part but because I fit the aesthetic, because my exterior fittingly chalk-outlines precisely what a "thug" is said to look like. So they place the name; they render me heated a priori, as if I'm always and already prepped to alleviate my internal madness and anger with nefarious plots. Even my father has stated that I am growing more aesthetically thug-like, namely because of my growing tattoo count, despite the fact that he has almost as many tattoos as I do. He who has known me my entire life even succumbs to the allure of defining a thug by external marks. If the man who is responsible for my existence can't even extricate popularly disseminated images of thuggishness from the uniqueness and, frankly, nerdiness of his only child, I wonder: What hope do I have when encountering the rest of the world?

As a matter of history's contingency, the extent to which my aesthetics congeal into an instantiation of Blackness does a kind of work. The "thug" might be read as some sort of disruption, a mutable disavowal of respectability that threatens to undo normative regimes. It is an irregularity sutured to an embodied Blackness. What I am interested in combing through here, briefly, is the nature of that irregularity—an irregularity I would call, as is my obsessive wont, a fugitivity—and its relation to, its being another name for, Blackness.

And I'm Black, but I'm most definitely known from the start.
— Mad Squablz, "Bar Fight"

Thug is black is nigger. America is nothing without its nigger.
— Mychal Denzel Smith, *Invisible Man,
Got the Whole World Watching*

I try to maintain a critical disposition, accounting for historical and socioeconomic reasons why certain ways of behaving, or certain postures of bravado, seem appealing in the first place. What utility does thuggishness serve? For what reason is it a characterization cast onto others, and for what reason is it lapped up by some? What conditions are present that would necessitate both the demonization of the figure of the thug and, simultaneously, its ravenous consumption? I wonder, in all seriousness, is it bad to be the thug? Is it even an identity that subjects willingly opt for? Is a thug somehow less than human, less than valuable, less than a valid subject? Sure, it's an identity that some people choose to inhabit, even flaunt, but I wonder if one seeks to enact thuggishness for itself. That is to say, echoing James Baldwin, we have in this country something called the thug, a consolidation of projected fears and the irruptive breach of social propriety. I did not invent the thug, but someone, someones, did. The language crafted to attach itself to those whose decorum—a decorum whose criteria are always determined by another—transgresses the threshold of the acceptable marks a strategy meant to uphold the order of things. The thug was made out of a fear of power's disintegration. One might then imagine, possibly, that those who enact the persona of the thug may be deploying it only insofar as it produces a particular effect, whether fear, respect, or a stratagem of survival in the cauldron of penury known popularly as "the ghetto."

Not only is this the case, but so, too, is the figure's fashioning used as a rationale for the extermination of those onto whom the figure is cast. One need not mourn the murder of a thug, it goes, as the thug (admittedly an overwhelmingly masculine term) was inevitably going to—if he hadn't done so already—commit some unconscionable act, whether jack your car, gun down an innocent child, mug an old lady, smoke a doobie, or burglarize your house. Hell, the thug may have been going to church, helping the sick and dying, volunteering at a homeless shelter, rescuing kittens from a burning building, donating to charity, or eating chocolate chip cookies. So long as the thug was given over to Blackness and thus, by virtue of that Blackness, *bound to* be on their merry way to do some dastardly deed, then it's only morally upstanding to eliminate the threat—the inevitable threat— before it strikes. As long as the name is placed, it follows that one will act in accordance with what that name signifies. And of course, who in their right mind would treat a thug well?

One might ask, What's in a name? If the names we are called and call ourselves speak us, in part, into social being, then to be called a thug matters. One structures one's perceptions and orientation to the world through language, which means that one extracts, or rather creates, meaning through the language used to describe and situate what one encounters. So, too, does one approach the thug with the intention of interacting with them as if their very being was characterized by this perceived thuggishness. And again, who would treat a thug well?

But what is a thug, really? The word *thug* has a history of imposition, forced poverty, racially motivated oppression, and image policing. The word comes from the Hindi and Mahratti words *ṭhag* and *ṭhak*, meaning a cheat or swindler. Historically, a thug is one of an association of professional robbers and murderers in India who strangled their victims. In the racially charged contemporary American context, a thug arises in relation to the way that Blackness has been made to consolidate the rough edges of the outside. Or rather, by way of Blackness's fugitivity, thuggishness becomes emblematic of fugitivity's deviance. Again we come to the effects of a fugitive penchant for subverting regimes of order and propriety affixing to, and coming to stand in as, Blackness. If "thug" often serves as a proxy for "nigger," it is because the dreaded epithet references a historical subject, to be sure, but more originarily because there is an unruly set of codes that govern other types of beings who want to be otherwise-than beings. I am interested in how that troubling thing that the thug, and more historically the nigger, serves to name denotes an outside to this stifling austerity that demands that we play by the rules. What if that thing, by way of its crammed propinquity to Blackness, signals a fugitive escape that provides a glimpse into another way, an other way, to be?

Now, while the violence enacted by those doing what thugs do is not to be praised or venerated (the fact remains that those who are marginalized in terms of race, gender, and sex are subject to the violence committed by those trying to maintain such behavior), of interest is the way that Criminality with a capital *C* is racialized and classed, which obscures the State-sanctioned criminality and violence masquerading as justice. We should already know that soaring rates of poverty and joblessness, dismally funded education, the influx of narcotics, and limited opportunities for recreation increase the rate of what has been classified as crime. These are conditions, though, that are the product of larger systems of relegation and disbursement. Put simply, people in particular neighborhoods are not as dangerous as the State-imposed, historically determined conditions constructing those neighborhoods. I wonder, then, what is the designated prison sentence for sequestering people in areas of perpetual poverty and poor resources for generations, or ensuring that folks are systematically disenfranchised and murdered based on racially coded optics of policing, surveillance, and profiling? Is it not criminal to essentially raise monsters for sport, nearly guaranteeing such a lack of opportunity that it necessitates criminal behavior, for which they are seen as so corrupt as to need to be exterminated? How inhumane is it—or in fact how thoroughly, thoroughly human?

So for me to be branded as a thug by friends, friends of friends, and even complete strangers based solely on my Blackness, "gangster" apparel, and physicality is for people's perception of me to be disciplined by that imposed identity. If I am called a thug, that means I am *seen* as a thug. The violence of this nonconsensual torquing of my subjectivity is visceral. If I am seen and labeled and identified as a thug, I am acted upon as such and, quite frankly, put in grave danger. To be called a thug, even by well-meaning loved ones, can unknowingly etch my name onto a slab of stone amid a sea of decomposed lives with memories and families they will never know again.

Thugs apparently don't do life correctly. They squander life, use it in a way it wasn't meant to be used, they say. The Black thuggish mode of being becomes existence manqué—existence gone wrong. Like an ungrateful and tantruming child, the thug is put in time-out, told to go to their room to think about what they've done. That room can look like a cell; time-out can last twenty-five years to life. You might not even get to suck the stale air of the prison-industrial complex. No more air for you; no more living, no more breath. Garner wasn't the only one gasping.

What, I ask again, is a thug really? Can thugs be, like me, feminists, scholars, writers, vegetarians, cartoon watchers, environmentalists? Can thugs be lachrymose babies when watching the end of a rom-com? Can thugs, in all their thuggish glory, love and dance and sing and marvel at the wondrousness of existence? Can they?

Can they, I ask you?

I'm unsure, and I hesitate to even give a definitive answer to this question of the thug, as they are indeed insurgent, social questions. What I know is that thugs have import, an import that has killed many, propelled some to fame, and restricted the flourishing of many others. Whether thugs primarily masquerade as such or have adopted the persona to such an extent that it has become who they are is not for me to decide here on my own. What is clear, though, is that thugs exist—wherever on the spectrum of artifice and authenticity, or outside of that very logic entirely—and, because of this, you better recognize.

Dawg Fights

'Cause we could put the guns down and go one round
With the hands, my man, I ain't the one, you'll get done,
clown.

— Big L, "You Know What I'm About"

The movie *Fight Club* initiated a wave of teenagers and twenty-somethings thinking they could whoop anyone's ass in their backyards. The people I hung out with in high school were no different. Two pairs of UFC gloves, a little bravado, no shirts, and you had yourself a good ol' fashioned fight club right there on the outskirts of Philly.

A group of friends and I were hanging out one summer day at one of their apartment buildings. John, our host, was starting basic training for the military in the coming days and he wanted his closest friends to come hang one last time. We barbecued and threw the football around, talked shit—the usual for us. Darkness rapidly fell upon us and people grew bored until someone suggested we, of all things, fight. I wasn't rushing to get my ass kicked or end up arrested, so I just sat there, my then girlfriend on my lap, and let them have at it.

Dante, a light-skinned dude who looked strikingly like Pharrell Williams, got the gloves from his car and John geared up to fight Darragh, a skinny surfer-looking jokester. Why Dante had the gloves waiting in his car in the first place, I am not sure, but apathy clutched me and I gave myself over to listening to the background brawl. While everyone else gathered in a crowd in the small grassy lot next to John's apartment building, my girlfriend and I were falling asleep in a lawn chair yards away, me listening and her already snoring lightly. I imagined punches were being thrown and missed, grins of levity traded in response to the fact that the fight was not about malice, reactions tailored to narrate the fight's trajectory. Then, "Oh shit!" they yelled, stopping the fight after John got choked out.

A little white kid named Pedro who had started lifting weights a couple months ago came over with his best friend Jeremy—just a little white kid—and jokingly said that they wanted to fight me. I wasn't enthused about the prospect of fighting, especially since I was comfortable and sleepy, my leg going numb with the weight of an entire person on top of it. But the people wanted to see the buff Black dude fight. More people came over and said that John would fight me (apparently everyone else was too chicken). I carried my still-sleeping girlfriend over to the lot, placed her on the hood of a car, waking her up, and agreed to fight John if only to shut everyone up. "Oh shit, Marquis is about to fight?" Kevin "Freak Nasty" asked. (His nickname was ironic since he was a portly, awkward virgin who was quite sexually repellent.) My closest high-school friends eagerly awaited the fight; their girlfriends and some other women some of them were trying to hook up with wanted to know what all the fuss was about. I strapped on my gloves and struggled to get my customized "Roidz" T-shirt off while my girlfriend came over to give me a good-luck kiss. I was nervous as hell, my mouth drier than ashy skin. I've never been in a real fight in my life and now I got a bunch of people expecting the big Black dude with tattoos to do his big Black fighting thing. Shit.

Our "ref," José, clapped his hands and the fight was on.

No punches were thrown for the first ten seconds; we just felt each other out. I switched my stance twice like an amateur. I swung and missed. He telegraphed a left hook and I ducked it, following up with a jab that landed. I got tapped on the left temple. Hit him with a body shot. Jab. Another jab. Two-piece and a biscuit. My brother always told me, when it comes to scrapping, to not swing all wild: *You stand there and box niggas.*

Because I wrestled in high school, I preferred groundwork. I took a shot, brought him down. Got his back, threw fists. José stood us up. The fight ended soon after, with me landing a flush superman punch to his nose.

This story is not really about this story. It is more about a series of moments in my life growing up around men, primarily though not exclusively, who brawled for a variety of reasons. Good and bad, if you'll allow such simplistic binary language. This is about the moments in my life when fisticuffs were more than mere pugilistic retribution or showboating, though they were often that. This is about what inchoate alternative forms of life might look like, and how they might, problematically at times, offer us all another way to live in this world.

I remember back in the day dudes used to square up not by throwing up their hands but by, of all things, touching shoulders. Like, my right chest and shoulder against yours, our heads sorta behind one another's. I found it hilarious, but never got why people did it. So I texted my brother, who's much more street-savvy than I.

> May 23 5:03 p.m.: Yo bro, this a really random question lol but you remember when dudes used to square up by pressing their shoulders against each other? Looked like hugging giraffes yo lol but did they have a name for that?
> May 23 5:08 p.m.: Ctfu basically trying to see who goin swing first and who intimidate who
> May 23 5:09 p.m.: Gotcha. That shit was hilarious lol
> May 23 5:10 p.m.: Lol I used to do that tho

I used to do that tho is my brother's nostalgia kicking in, a nostalgia not for being young and squaring up with others but for an experimental levity (note the "Lol"). Now with two kids and a very dad-esque body, his priorities are not all that have shifted; so have his horizons. *Lol I used to do that tho* is a reminiscence about how rubrics of evaluation were not always those of the working world and capitalist ventures. Those other rubrics that made my brother "lol" operated according to other sets of rules and inquiries: You can outsmart me, outrun me, trash me on the ball court, take my girl, make more money than me, and diss my mom, but can you rumble? Can you see me in the streets? Do those hands get busy? If we went toe to toe right now, would you leave leaking? If you couldn't put your dukes up and handle me in the streets too, the rest didn't matter.

(I feel like I need to make a disclaimer: I am uninterested in conveying an endorsement of violence in this and my subsequent meditation. I am uninterested in touting how much pain one can inflict on another as an accurate, or desirable, measure of one's masculinity or toughness. In truth, I care very little about either masculinity or toughness as barometers of anything good. Largely, I do not think they are. What I am doing here and throughout the essay is cultivating a discursive space for others to convey how they understand, and are forced to understand, the world into which they were thrown. While surely there are other understandings, these, whether I like it or not, might be an inchoate example of people who thoroughly live by goon rules. This is an inscription of their goon story.)

Capturing the sentiments of those whom I grew up with is the documentary *Dawg Fight* (2015). The film documents a crime-plagued neighborhood near Miami where brutal, bare-knuckled backyard fights give young men a chance to earn money and self-respect. Fights end in one of three ways: by knockout, referee stoppage, or quitting. No hits to the back of the head, no groin strikes. But really, only one rule truly matters: "Don't give up. Fight yo' fight, nigga. Fight yo' fight."

The film opens with a definition. Rakontur—the name of the production company and a modified spelling of *raconteur*—is, they write, a "n. one who tells stories with skill." The film is indeed a story told with dexterity. It is the story, the narrative, of people who do not have the means to tell their own stories. The focal character, Dhafir "Dada 5000" Harris, has been running backyard fights for almost two years, and the fights' YouTube traffic has led to a few fighters being recognized and signed professionally. Dada began in the twelve-by-twelve ring himself, fighting and winning against various opponents, and at one point ran security for and fought alongside Kimbo Slice's professional team. (Kimbo Slice also got his professional start after becoming a YouTube sensation. Slice, in fact, grew up "right down the street" from Dada.) Dada is a big dude, weighing over 260 pounds and benching over 650. Described by his aunt as "real rugged and rough," Dada stopped fighting for Slice's team because they weren't releasing any of his footage (presumably, according to Dada, because it would take the spotlight off of Slice: "It was that destructive," he says), and he stopped fighting for a while altogether because in his last fight, against a man named Chauncy who was fresh out of prison and hopped up on morphine, he left his opponent's face nearly unrecognizable. "Dhafir got a heart," Dada's aunt, Ellenor Stewart, says. "He's got a conscience."

The backyard fights were designed to "[give] back to the 'hood.... We giving them alternative means of solving conflicts." Alternative means, other and othered and otherwise means to a more ethical sociality. Many of the participants, along with only being able to train in their own backyards with makeshift equipment and scraps from junkyards, have criminal records. They carry with them their criminality. But it's a different kind, *the necessary deregulation and the possibilities of criminality and fugitivity that labor upon labor requires; the anoriginary drive and the insistences it calls into being and moves through.*[1] *That* criminality. Living in impoverished Perrine, Florida, in Miami-Dade County, and being Black and deprived of educational resources, many of them have no opportunities outside of selling drugs, theft, or fighting. Perrine is a suburban ghetto of sorts. It is 63 percent Black. The unemployment rate is over a third higher than the national average, and poverty and crime are rampant. Thus, like Dada says at the Martin Luther King parade, "Alotta individuals don't know about Perrine. They know about Miami but they don't know about the dark side. We are the dark side. This is where dreams are lost and hope is diminished. This is the bottom." This, one might say, is the undercommons.

Where they are, which is both where they have been forced to be and where they choose to remain, is an undercommon community; the dark underside, the subterranean lowdown where the work grinds on in secrecy and volatile hushed tones. A space that they occupy because they are preoccupied with it; a Black Market space with an illegible economy of different kinds of goods that are traded and bartered freely in exchange for the sociality that happens in the trading and bartering. It might be that Perrine, Florida, as an undercommons, is not where people do particular things—trekking to work, doing business, walking the dog—but is instead where work gets done, a distinction characterized by an experimentation with another mode of life. A fugitive mode of life, in the vicinity of criminality, but a robust criminality, a disposition to live another way that breaks metaphysical laws of this being the only way. Perrine's undercommonality is a sensibility, an occupied and preoccupied elsewhere that is right here. And eruptions often occur.

Though on their surface they are rather violent and dangerous, and potentially glorify such a lifestyle, the backyard brawls serve a very particular purpose in the community. The backyard fights are "for those who don't have a résumé but have a rap sheet." The backyard fights were envisioned to settle disputes without grabbing a gat and popping one off in somebody's skull. Quite frankly, as Dyrushio Harris says, "we sick of burying good dudes, man." "If you got a beef with somebody you can always come to the backyard and settle it." Therein, perhaps, lies the greatest value of these fights. Beef-settling by other means, conceptualizing differently how we might live together.

The fighting is rarely an act of malice or retribution proliferating harm in a neighborhood mired in harm. It is possible, they show, for there to be another understanding of violence that is not invalidated by the mere existence of swollen eyes and spilled blood. Understand it, the fighting, as an alternative mode of inaugurating one's subjectivity. It is an ethical otherwise way of being in the community, a surface violence that mitigates the possibility of a deeper violence. Unlike my scrap in the yard of John's apartment building, which served only to soothe our boredom, in Perrine these fighting "dawgs" fight because they are so very tired of fighting.

But I have to confess, to you and to myself, that viewing these men— Michael Anthony "K.O. Mike" Trujillo, Sylvester "Fruity" Squire III, Chanza "Chauncy" Adside, Lamorick "Moe" Moore, Treon "Tree" Johnson—was akin to watching an embodied musical symphony, or an expertly choreographed ballet with beautiful contusions and majestic lacerations. They were making music in the ring—perverse, ghetto, Black music; music that hurt, music that was indecorous, music that knocked out your gold grill, music that dropped your ass unconscious with a right hook. Sing for me, left jab; croon for us, uppercut. Its allure enticed me, seduced my gaze into wanting to look more deeply, across and beyond and to the side of the surface of the infliction of harm. I'm not completely sure if this elsewhere-looking is justified, but it is nevertheless illuminating.

In that twelve-by-twelve ring made of flimsy poles jammed into the dirt of an unkempt lawn, spatially reduced to eliminate running and encourage confrontation, these men exorcised demons. Perhaps it is no coincidence that in a strange way I felt like I was at a Black church. A burly Black man stood front and center, bellowing commands with a sagacity that defied his age; bodies in motion connoted something divine occurring; and whether the call was a "Can I get an 'Amen'?"

or a flush punch, the response was an eruption of emotion or a terse call-back to "fuck that nigga up!" letting everyone know that we are all here, we are all a part of this community, we are all feeling this with you. The incomprehensibility of someone waking up from a knockout or of the way the body moved so quickly, fluidly, and yet not entirely of one's own accord was an indecipherable language, a tonguelike speech, a ghetto glossolalia.

So much like the Black church, which was in many ways African Americans' salvation in the trying times of de jure and de facto segregation and white supremacy, these backyard brawls were, oddly enough, a haven of solace for participants and spectators alike. Fruity, aka "Problem Child," could have been on the 1996 Olympic boxing team but went to prison for eight years on charges of armed robbery. He says that "basically, since I been rolling with Dada I been out the street." If opportunities in the community and larger society are scarce, especially for these Black men, many of whom have felonies, the chance to do at least one thing they know how to do—throw down with the fists—and earn money doing it can very much be the difference between life and death. For some, fighting is the only alternative to gangbanging or selling drugs, with Tree pointing out that "I ain't wanna sell no drugs, so I just started doing what I knew how to do [fighting]."

And the payoff can be much more than the three to four hundred dollars winners leave with. In an era when YouTube views are a form of currency, backyard brawls are inspiring a new generation of people to fight their way out of the ghetto. ("We doing something that George W. Bush failed to do," one of the Harris twins avers. "We bringin' jobs back.") They're fighting for a chance at a better livelihood. It's "all love. This is motherfuckin' business. This shit ain't personal." The fights are not senseless acts of violence but meaningful forms of racial and gendered validation, economic restoration, community building, and self-assessment. These fights are worthy of tears.

But aside from the action in the ring and extralegal action in the streets, the four women who served as post-fight commentators—Janice Riggins, Christine Prescott, Ramona King, and Kelli "Lobo" Andrews—were one of the most intriguing components of the film. Their commentary was raw: "Jimmy is a punk. He is a puuunk," one said after the fight between James "Jimmy" Thompson and Tree. "Tree is a fuckin' clown!" said another. This was Black women giving the final say on the effect and value of each fight; Black women speaking their realities, their standpoint theories, into validity from the comfort of lawn chairs. With them, there was no technical analysis of the fighters' training, technique, or strategy, just, "He is a soldier. That boy didn't give up even though his eye was like this, his lip was down here. . . ."; "The fight was off the chain"; "Now *that right there* was a fight." After the much-anticipated fight between Tree and Chauncy in which the women unanimously championed Chauncy's inevitable victory, one woman said, "See, I told you. I told you. Didn't I tell you that?" This preemptive declaration of Chauncy's win, though it had not yet happened when they foretold his victory, is an instantiation of what grammarians would call future real conditional tense, or that which will have had to happen for the future to be realized, a future that hasn't yet happened but must. It is a Black feminist grammar, the idea of living the future *now*, or imagining what must be and embodying that idea in the present. Thus the women lived a necessary future by speaking its reality, requiring only that viewers' recognition of their prescience be ensured. *Didn't I tell you that?*

Though the focus of the film is on the Black men whose physiques get physical in the ring, Black women function as authoritative subjects not through physicality but via speech acts (my mother's *'Cause I said so* echoes loudly, and viscerally, here). Riggins, Prescott, King, and Andrews give the "final" word on the fights; Ellenor Stewart gives the go-ahead necessary for the fights to even occur, since they occur in her backyard; after Lamorick "Moe" Moore loses his fight to Chauncy, Moe's girlfriend puts the kibosh on him ever fighting again, saying to Dada, "He ain't fighting no more. . . . He got fucked up"; and when Jimmy ends his fight with Tree because he thinks Dada is cheating him, Jimmy's girlfriend throws a fit, sealing the "truth" of the occurrence of cheating. So I can put it to you like this: nothing gets done, nothing is officially finished, and nothing is verified without the say-so of a Black woman. Damn, how true this was growing up in my house. Mom didn't give you the go-ahead or Grandma didn't say it was cool, then it ain't go down. Let somebody disobey that declaration, and it would not . . . end . . . well. Ask my brother.

So I wonder, as I so often do, being one who fancies himself a philosopher: Who had the power? You got these jacked dudes trading blows to the face and getting as bloody as Carrie at the prom, but how powerful is it to have your will manifest without lifting a finger? "Power doesn't have to show off," Ralph Ellison penned in his canonical *Invisible Man*.

But all was not always well. Such can be expected when engaging with the undercommons' Blackness, when its minor-key sensibilities are made major, put right there for all to see yet not caring who the hell is doing the seeing. Fugitive gatherings and devious assemblages draw the attention of forces of governance and control. Enter Dada's manager and fight promoter, Thomas Molloy:

> Fighting in the backyards or in the streets or warehouses—wherever they find their places to fight—it's unsanctioned, and unsanctioned means that you have non-qualified referees, judges. No physicians. Participating, you can get a second-degree misdemeanor for it; as a promoter you could get a third-degree felony charge on it. Somebody gets killed there, there's gonna be two people going to jail at least, for murder, and that would be the fighter that fought him and killed him, and the promoter who put the fight on.

He acts as the mouthpiece for hegemonic control, which makes all the participants in backyard fighting—fighters, promoters, and spectators—literal fugitives. They have rap sheets and, since they continue backyard fighting, they practice a continual refusal of the terms of the Law, undermining the very codes and regulations that insist on the illegality and unsanctionability of the fights. Their Blackness, which extends far, renders unanswerable the question of how to govern their bodies. They defy the logic of correction—there is nothing to correct because even though someone like Molloy lists the litany of laws one breaks when engaging in street fighting, Dada still concludes, on behalf of all those in Miami-Dade County, that "what he [Molloy] believes is not reality where I come from." Thus Molloy's regulative mode of operating in the world is ill-fitted to the world Dada comes from—indeed, they play by different rules. Perrine's undercommonality plays by outlaw and out-of-law rules, rebel rules, *goon rules*. Dada and all those participating in the backyard fights usurp the regulative, governing force of (the) Law.

But with the subversiveness and incisiveness that *Dawg Fight*'s cast embodies, all that's well does not end well. Two months after Chauncy and Tree's fight, Chauncy was shot in the back of his head by his girlfriend's brother, Charlton, after an altercation they had one night. Chauncy tried to walk away from the situation, but Charlton—who, convicted of second-degree murder, died of a heart attack just months into his fifteen-year sentence—grabbed a .22 caliber pistol and shot Chauncy, shattering Chauncy's number-two vertebrae. Kept on life support for a brief period of time, Chauncy had his plug pulled.

And Tree, who reminded Dyrushio Harris of Muhammad Ali because he "got the fight game and talk game on lock," died at twenty-seven years old after being tasered and pepper-sprayed by Hialeah police on February 27, 2014.

These deaths occurred not in the ring where the men were being pummeled but out in the world where the pummeling too often goes unnoticed. The comments about the film on Netflix are peppered with disapproval of the violence and thought-to-be glorification of unregulated fighting, but what goes conspicuously unmentioned is the constant assault these subjects endure via militarized police presence, cyclical poverty, the severed images of their own Black bodies returned to them after being chewed by white representational gazes, and negative connotations ascribed to Miami-Dade County when it is not erased altogether.

So yes, fight clubs happen way more often than you'd think. The backyards, warehouses, basements, or empty lots are where you might go to see what would happen if you found yourself in the ring with yourself. Condemn it all you want because it's violent, unsafe, illegal. Fine. But ask yourself: How big is the club? How expansive is the warehouse, the backyard, the lot? So quick are we to cast aspersions on unsanctioned fisticuffs but we flock to boxing and MMA fights. Or better yet, think how quickly we rush to YouTube and Netflix comments, strutting our self-righteous liberalism, but fail to think about how the fight doesn't end for those bodies after they step out of the ring. It is in fact outside the ring that the fight club takes place, and those well-known rules are enforced with imprisonment, ghettos, shots to the back, hoses, dogs, the rope and knot, and the auction block. The first rule: don't talk about Fight Club (Black lives); the second rule: don't talk about Fight Club (white lies).

REFUSAL

Exhaustive celebration of and in and through our suffering, which is neither distant nor sutured, is black study. That continually rewound and remade claim upon our monstrosity—our miracle, our showing, which is neither near nor far, as [Hortense] Spillers shows—is black feminism, the animaterial ecology of black and thoughtful stolen life as it steals away.

— Fred Moten, *Black and Blur* ·

The ALP Journals

For a few months I worked alongside the Audre Lorde Project (ALP), a New York–based social justice organization focusing on community organizing for queer and trans/gendernonconforming folks of Color; I spent these months thinking in coalitional solidarity with its TransJustice Division, learning primarily from Nico Fonseca and Jamal Lewis, and hopefully providing some knowledge and insight myself. When doing such work, it is crucial to position oneself not as an agent of governmentality—"I'm from the Institution and I'm going to help you, you poor thing"—but rather as a service worker, one who has been gifted access to a sacred space and is willing to put one's aptitudes to work in the service of communities. The following entries document both the collective knowledge production during my meetings with the ALP and the thinking that arose in response to my proximity to ALP's gender justice work. These entries, at base, are reflections on the import of Blackness and radical gender politics. These entries are, following Du Bois, "a number of my fugitive pieces."

September 5, 2017

Pronouns: Jamal (Jamal), Nico (they/them), Me (he/him; they/them)*
The work, perhaps by necessity, will be difficult. It is the work of abolition because it is trans/gender justice, and abolition is a radical, and radically difficult, constant struggle. I've been trying to meditate deeply on what gender is and what gender does, and what function the "alphabet soup" of gendered appellations serves. As I said during our meeting, in agreement with both Jamal and Nico, the ever-elongating LGBTQQIATS . . . is not mere political correctness with respect to gender identification but, quite literally, gives people space to live. These designations are vital ways for folks to inhabit themselves, to survive in the world, to permit themselves to *be*.

Initially I found myself complaining about the four-hour drive to Jersey to catch the ferry to meet with ALP every two weeks, then the four-hour drive after the meeting back home. But this, I chided myself, is a small part of the work; it is striking that my "problems" are driving a few hours while those for whom I seek to put myself in service have ontological problems such as being misgendered, physical problems such as facing the fatal possibility of transantagonistic violence, financial problems such as not being able to buy food. Marquis, you better take several seats. Put in the work, do the service you claim you want to do, and drive the biweekly eight hours for the sake of gender justice.

I was particularly excited about the "Decolonizing Gender" zine or think-piece idea, as it captures one of my more potent interests: writing, and more specifically writing radically, about gender. As a quick loose reflection on the very idea of decolonizing gender: if

---

* And these designations are, as always, subject to change—tomorrow, in a month, a year from now.

colonization is a practice of claiming sovereignty over a population, of imposing a template onto a disparate, perhaps even joyously unruly terrain, then decolonizing gender strikes me as a perpetual practice of undoing such impositions and living gendered life—or maybe even living life ungendered insofar as "gender" is itself a hegemonic regime from which decolonization and abolition seek to extricate us—in subversion of these impositions.

"I'm inspired by the example of people of color who want to abolish the social construct of race, or working class people who want to abolish the social construct of capitalism. I want to abolish the social construct of patriarchy. I don't really see a way in which this could happen without also abolishing gender."

— A Radical Transfeminist, "Some Thoughts on Gender Abolition"

September 19, 2017

We tell stories, tell *our* stories, perhaps fundamentally because we want to live. Telling stories is a fundamental way in which we reveal to ourselves who we are and whence we come—and, even more fundamentally, that we exist, impossible as that may seem for some of us. It is this sentiment, it seems to me, that motivates the urge to collect stories, particularly of marginalized folks, folks whose stories have been willfully ignored, erased, obliterated, mischaracterized, gaslighted, and the like. I wonder, quite seriously, what trans stories might look and sound like. If we have been conditioned to understand the "storyness" of stories through the erasure of those stories that don't measure up and through the characterization of white, cis, male, etc., etc., etc. as the only stories worth the name, then how will trans stories—and trans people telling their own stories—force us to rethink how we understand stories? Are we ready for trans and *transed* stories? Really, are we?

Gender justice. That is, for me, where I might add my most potent contribution to this dope ALP trans and abolitionist foray. In speaking with Jamal, and about Jamal's vision for gender justice, we both, perhaps inevitably, spoke from the intellectual template of the Combahee River Collective's Black Feminist Statement. We must, because it is everything. And more pointedly with respect to the gender justice statement for ALP, how do we succinctly and accessibly (I'm always ambivalent about this term, its connotative valuation, its presumptive hubris) answer the question: What does a progressive, radical gender justice vision look like? This is the question Jamal posed to me, Jamal and all of ALP. So, a series of very brief, loose, and haphazard thoughts: self-determination and abolition.

Eradication of imposed discipline and the policing of others' gendered identifications—the arrogant claims that, as both Nico and Jamal shared in relation to those who disrespect their trans/gendered identifications, one is not "trans enough." (Which then made me think, what might it mean for one to refuse to be "cis enough," insofar as cisness rests on relational tenets of superiority, "naturalness," and violence?)

Expansion of the gendered lexicon—the gender "alphabet soup"—is not a mere hodgepodge of politically correct inclusiveness; it is the ever-expansion of livelihood, the cultivation of more room to simply breathe within oneself.

We are *and do* our genders, or perhaps are our genders *because* we do them, which also means that to whatever extent our genders are deemed "normative" we must choose, as an ethical and radical gesture, to do them wrongly, to refuse to play by normative rules, to go by other rules, by devious goon rules; to be bad gendered subjects.

The most radical gesture one can make regarding gender identification is to self-determine it. Rather than being on some rugged individualist tip, gender self-determination—or undetermination—seems to in fact be a coalitional move. We definitely enact a radically open and autonomous declaration of who we wish to be on each occasion that we self-determine and choose how we wish to "show up" in the world. But, too, it is a demand placed on us all to ensure that self-determinative spirit for others as well, to come at them with an utter, terrifying openness, presuming nothing, letting them show us as much or as little of themselves as they wish. This is how we form a different world worth living within: the radicality of all this movement work we're doing rests in the ability to be fractured and critiqued by the forgotten, to give oneself, radically open, to the unknownness of the other, and to accept as a gift the various iterations of "Y'all need to get y'all act together."

It is on the grounds that I do not know you in advance of you determining yourself and then graciously sharing that with me that we can live lovingly with one another. Self-determination is fundamental to quite simply finding a way to stay alive.

September 27, 2017

I've been thinking a bit about the function of an immensely complex but rhetorically simple question: "What pronoun do you prefer?" Nico, a couple meetings ago, mentioned how often this question resounds shallowly, as if asked as a mere nicety or perfunctory question by those who wish to be perceived as "woke." (Oh how I'm beginning to loathe this term, its platitudinous weight, its misguided finality.) And this happens often, unfortunately. While of course there are those who might ask it and immediately tune out, unconcerned with the response and caring only for their feminist / social justice woke-ness badge, I've been meditating a bit on the impact of the question. *What pronoun do you prefer?* I, for one, prefer either/both he-him-his and they-them-their, pronouns over which I am still mulling, unsure if they adequately capture my pursuit of unnormed and queered cis-ness. Put differently, and related to my previous entry, the uncertainty of my pronouns speaks to my constant pursuit to *fail* doing cisness, to be a bad cis subject, to queer—to whatever extent—not only what cisness might physically look like (which is what?) but the behaviors and tenets that one is coerced to *do* when believing, and encountering others who believe, that one is cis. Might even the question itself be doing work to this end: destabilizing the assumption of cisnorma-tivity, querying ever-shifting gender identifications and refusing to presume that we ever "know"?

But, again, the question: What pronoun do you prefer? The ques-tion strikes me as at once a way to abolish at least the assumption of a particular gender identity, a commitment to self-determination, and a lifeline. Asking the question maintains, implicitly, that we are comfortable with not knowing; indeed, that we are committing to a constant posture of not knowing, cultivating room for others to deter-mine themselves without being foreclosed by gendered assumptions. It is a constant openness to being undone. *What pronoun do you pre-fer?* is perhaps one way among many to say, "No, I *don't* see you, and that's okay because it is on your terms and in your language that you reveal yourself to me."

"There is no such thing as 'trans enough' or some sort of magic milepost at which you are suddenly given your gender entry visa and approved for maleland or femaleland."

— s. e. smith, "Beyond the Binary: Yes, Nonbinary Femmes Exist"

October 3, 2017

I read the ALP statement that was released after the shooting at the Pulse nightclub in Orlando on June 12, 2016. As ALP was constructing it, I sent a text to Danny—one of my closest comrades, a slim gay man whose intellectual mischievousness bespeaks a cunning fugitivity over which I repeatedly swoon—telling him that I loved him, that he was and had long been a member of my queer kinfolk. I sent a text to Kai M. Green, a Black trans man who continues to demonstrate that love is unbounded. I told him that he is (inherently) valuable, that he is loved. These are moments of eluding capture, of living life on the run. These are the moments Miss Major noted, moments where we are "chased but not caught," because we cannot be—because we refuse to be.

The statement demonstrated considerable breadth in its specificity, but Jamal noted, convincingly, that there is a trend to deploy "people of Color" in a way that both flattens the heft of anti-Blackness and lacks genuine specificity in the hopes of an uncritical inclusiveness. I noted Jared Sexton's essay "People-of-Color-Blindness," which speaks to this very point: the widespread and loose deployment of "PoC" becomes "a form of colorblindness inherent to the concept of 'people of color' to the precise extent that it misunderstands the specificity of antiblackness and presumes or insists upon the monolithic character of victimization under white supremacy."[1] In other words, Jamal was hinting at the fundamentality of Blackness, not "Coloredness," to anti-queer violence. What's more, as I went to leave for the day, telling Jamal about my love for ALP in relation to other New York–based social justice orgs, I went to use the word *intersectional* but caught myself, after which Jamal caught me catching myself. "I fucking hate that word," Jamal said. Yes, I do too, because it tries but always fails to be *Black*. Intersectional feminism is (or tries to be) and comes from Black feminism. But, I'd say unashamedly, Black feminism always does it better. Intersectional feminism is nice for sure, but it seems often like a more palatable diminishment of the radicality of Black feminism. And I would venture, also, to say that Jamal and I would agree: *Black* then becomes a term that names a radical mode of interrogating and subverting power, a queer political radicality rather than "just" a physical descriptor. The intersectional has served us very well, many-a-times; what happens at the meeting point of various vectors of how we understand (and how others understand) our identities is of significant consequence. But I wanna know more than what's happening at the intersection of Crenshaw and Elm. I wanna know what's going on in the sewers, how hot it is out here, and what they're yelling from the window. Focus on the intersections does not cover this breadth. But Blackness does.

We spoke of intimacy. Indeed, these conversations are intimate moments, differently intimate, but intimate nonetheless. We are sharing ourselves, being and becoming vulnerable in our thoughts, putting our lives into space to be handled with care or malice. How, Jamal queried, can we think about *intimate* protests? So many protests happen *out there* with bullhorns, shouts, stomping feet, and the fanfare of the spectacle. And this, no doubt, is valuable. To grieve and lament publicly, loudly, is a testament to the insistence on the mattering of Black life, Black queer life, Black trans life; it is a refusal to let the dead die. But is it possible, and what kind of different work can it do, to protest privately? What if, Jamal asked, we knew Pookie down the street was beating on his girlfriend, and the whole block showed up at his door and demanded redress and collective healing? What effect would a private, quiet—but no less loud, paradoxically enough—protest have?

The answer to this, one I am not competent enough yet to think of, might be the kind of justice carceral abolitionists aim for, justice that is not interested in meting out punishments but in facilitating healing.

Again, as always, when we think and do gender justice, radical gender work, we come to abolition in some form.

"Abolition must be one of the centers of trans and queer liberation struggles. . . . Among the most volatile points of contact between state violence and one's body is the domain of gender."

— Eric A. Stanley, "Fugitive Flesh: Gender Self-Determination,
Queer Abolition, and Trans Resistance"

October 10, 2017

It is just about impossible for me to think radical gender politics outside of the Black radical tradition. I thought out loud about a yearning for the otherwise, for "otherwise than being," as the philosopher Emmanuel Levinas would say, a way to inhabit ourselves in a radically different way, illegible to current scripts of embodiment. Jamal said Jamal made a short film titled "Otherwise Gendered," and I got giddy. I am curious—always curious, thinking, perhaps, otherwise—about how it might be possible to understand our genders otherwise; curious about how we might do gender differently, how we might enact genders as on the run from hegemony. I want, I think, *fugitive genders.* Fugitive genders might be what arise in the rubble of the life that happens subsequent to gender abolition. Fugitive genders are those genders that might arise but for the hegemonic regime of "Gender," self-determinative and agential subjectivity that refuses to be bounded.

It is difficult for me to reconcile this, or simply to think it in tandem, with the question of historical ethics. That is, what happens in this radical thinking of gender abolition when there are those who hold steadfastly to the genders they've inherited and justifiably balk at the suggestion to now hold them in contempt? Is there room for one to clutch at cis womanhood while aiding the insurgent politics to abolish the deleterious effects of gender's regime? Does it leave an unpleasant taste on our pink papillae to grant uncritical validity to any gender one wishes to hold?

A radical gender politics that reaches for the otherwise-genders is an undoing of fundamental bedrocks of whom we have come to believe we are. And it is terrifying, holding the potential for both the dangerously reactive and the dangerously revolutionary. The extent to which we continue to rest our heads comfortably in the normative constitutive tenets of imposed genders is the extent to which we uphold the empire. Can we extract the portions of the corrosive regime of gender that delight us and affirm us without upholding the entire empire? I grapple with even daring to provide an answer. Nevertheless, maintaining the empire involves acquiescing to the notions of a proper person and proper embodiment, as these have as their grounding the gender binary and unbreachable tenets of male = masculine = man / female = feminine = woman. I wonder, in timid quiet moments, whether what we want to do in our radical work is undermine and undo the world.

We cannot think radical trans axioms of abolition and self-determination outside of Black radicality. On the grounds that Blackness is necessarily a rattling of gender's edges, and on the grounds that "abolition" is saturated with a history of proximity to and inception within the volatile effects of Blackness, to do gender otherwise, to hold but not possessively have fugitive gender, is to reckon with Blackness and its proximity to queerness and transness.

"To center radical black, anticolonial, and prison abolitionist traditions is to already be inside trans politics."
— Eric A. Stanley, "Gender Self-Determination"

November 1, 2017

I dislike, vehemently, the term *ally*. This is not to say that I do not want white folks doing work to dismantle white supremacy, cis folks fighting transantagonism, or (cis) men undoing male supremacist patriarchy. Not at all. All of this is absolutely welcome, to be sure. My beef, as it were, is with how "allyship" is mobilized in problematic ways—namely, as a way to maintain and in fact foreground one's hegemonic identification. For one to consistently tout their allyship and do that dance of "acknowledging their privilege" keeps intact the integrity of that identity rather than doing the work to destroy it. To be an ally becomes a political identity in itself, and a somewhat shallow one, as it becomes the purview from which one does one's politics: not as someone "in the struggle" but as someone outside the struggle, cheering it on and shouting about how white/cis/male/straight/etc./etc./etc. they are, which means—*shrug*—that y'all do the work while I stand over here watching.

I showed a video to my Feminist Essays class last semester interrogating the notion of allyship. It provided a newer, more radical term for those typically known as allies: *accomplices*. The aim, at least for me, is not to say that the aforementioned people should not be doing the subversive work they are doing (to the extent that it in fact *is* subversive) but to place more of a demand on them. Allies are still loved. We love us our white folks, our cis men. Folks like William Lloyd Garrison, John Brown, the Grimké sisters—yes, gimme them any day; gimme Tim Wise and Andrea Gibson. They bring wreck to white and male supremacy—because they are accomplices, co-conspirators. Accomplices are traitors to their apparent epidermal (and gendered) allegiances. Co-conspirators uptake the *work* that is entailed in the Black radical tradition, a thoroughly radical feminist tradition, and enact deviancy in spite of the coercion to believe that they are in fact rightfully at the top of the proverbial food chain. They occupy the "place of the demand," as Kai M. Green puts it in our forthcoming conversation on the meeting ground of Black feminism and trans feminism—that is, the fertile ground on which we must all do the radical, revolutionary work not only *from* but *despite* and *in excess of* where we are. To be deemed an accomplice, or alternatively a co-conspirator, means that one drives the getaway car from the scene of the queer, feminist, Black radical crime; it means that one dwells in deviancy with the misfits and outlaws.

To be sure, this is difficult work. We will fail, succumb to the allure of normativity, be seduced by hegemony, but it is the perpetual taking up of the demand to become and pursuit of becoming otherwise than the hegemonic selves we are told we must believe we are (and will always be) that characterizes fugitive work of the co-conspiratorial variety. I've been told that this does a disservice to communities that wish to "self-segregate" into safe spaces away from corporeal instanti- ations of the violent supremacies that exist. "Allyship" has as a benefit that white folks, dudes, cis folks, and straight folks know not to invade spaces designated strictly for a specific marginalized demographic. I get this. And these spaces are important. My only response—an incomplete and thoroughly inexhaustive response—is to ask what it is that we wish to rally around. How do we find coalition with others: on the grounds of hurt, subjection to violence, historical trauma? Is it also possible to rally around, in the first instance, our commitment to undoing and dismantling hegemonic power? Can we rally around, in the first instance (and not to the exclusion of other points of connec- tion, of which subjection or trauma might be one), the kind of world in which we want to live? Can we, finally, rally around how intensely we seek to bring this muhfucka down, and can that intensity become the means by which we find kinship?

These are musings, and incomplete ones, subject to change. But as musings, they are provocations that, I hope, are ultimately in service of making the world livable for those who are said to have no life to live here.

November 6, 2017

"Riffing," as a verb, comes from popular music, specifically jazz. It's an improvisation, a serial introduction and reintroduction of a theme, a variation and reworking of something. To riff is to care for the inability to get something completely, comprehensively down. It is a love of incompleteness, a love of getting outside of it all and doing it again. A love of perpetual self-unmastery. A love of that thing that's always getting away from you, that illegible, slippery thing that lovingly mocks you because the both of you know it's all love.

I want to riff on a passage that has enraptured me since I first read it. It is a passage that bears a referential relationship to that other one, that "Middle" one, that has set in motion an oceanic proliferation of perverse richness and destructive creativity. I want to riff on something Black trans studies scholar C. Riley Snorton writes in his book *Black on Both Sides: A Racial History of Trans Identity*, just because and not at all just because; just because and, at the same time, for every possible reason that matters:

> To suppose that one can identify fugitive moments in the hollow of fungibility's embrace is to focus on modes of escape, of wander, of flight that exist within violent conditions of exchange. Transitive—as in fungible passing into fugitive—and transversal—as in fugitivity intersecting fungibility, this . . . explores the fugitive (and at once fungible) narratives of black people—born free or into captivity—in the era of slavery's formal transition. Here, the transitivity and transversality of fungibility and fugitivity find expression in a line of a poem by Fred Moten, wherein the figures under principal review . . . "ran from it and [were] *still* in it." Fugitive narratives featuring "cross-dressed" and cross-gender modes of wander and escape, most often described in terms of "passing," function as a kind of map for a neglected dimension of what [Hortense] Spillers defined as the semiotic terrain of black

bodies under captivity, wherein gender refers not to a binary system of classification but to a "territory of cultural and political maneuver, not at all gender-related, gender-specific."[2]

I always want to focus on modes of escape, though I know why some folks prefer the inverse, to focus on how we ain't free. The pressure of captivity is real and it's little surprise that, because of this unbearable, indomitable realness, it's primarily what some folks want to talk about. But, nevertheless, I want to talk about escape, about getting outside of it, about capacity to move out over there because, well, I wanna talk about it.

What Snorton is getting at, and what I think is relevant to these pages and the general spirit of the ALP and the gender justice we are seeking, is that gender, when encountering and getting cozy with Blackness, is a fundamental fugitivity—a fundamental escape and "*capacity* under captivity," as Snorton says elsewhere—that is enabled by Blackness's transitivity (meaning its existence as a generative mutability), Blackness's deployment of fungibility and fugitivity. Gender is always political and politicized, and Blackness's manifestations of gender transgression bear this out since Blackness, through historical and social placement outside the categorical regime of gender's binaristic henchpeople, runs from gender. As it should. So let's take note.

Snorton also writes something radically insightful later in his book. Noting very seriously that it is becoming widely understood in more radical trans spaces that "trans embodiment is not exclusively, or even primarily, a matter of the materiality of the body," that there are "other ways to be trans," he implies that transness becomes distinct from being transgender and in fact references subversive movement, deviantly rogue movement, excess that spills over the confines of normativity. If we concede, as Snorton says at the very outset of *Black on Both Sides*, that the transness of one's gender should not "in this instance (or any, for that matter) . . . be adjudicated by making recourse to the visual," we are tasked with suspending our commitment to thinking that we know, instantly, one's gender. That suspension might lead us to an elsewhere location which might express itself in aberrance and in subversive relation to normativity. To do trans and transed gender, which is, multiplicitously, how gender always manifests, is always a criminal commitment to deviancy.

Blackness and its devious play with gender, which is to say fugitivity, provide a map for how we might find a way out of this trap; it might help us work and put this trap to work toward its own destruction. It will be hard, for sure, but if liberation is the name of the game we want to play, this is the work required: fugitive escape, in and through the cartographically blessed sign of Blackness's troubling of gender, in which we might finally end this nightmare.

November 14, 2017

I've been thinking more about pronouns, but a bit differently. Often the subject comes up with trans or genderqueer or nonbinary folks—grown folks—who can autonomously determine their own gender pronouns and correct you if you misgender them. And, too, these pronouns are chosen, and can change, based on how that person wishes to identify, which is to say how that person wants to exist in the world in that moment. But my brother has an eighteen-month-old, Chase, an adorable kid prone to stealing Grandma's socks off her feet and running away laughing, and Grandma always says, rightly, that Chase is "slick." Chase is joyous about life and can dance the day away while watching *Sesame Street* (and don't you dare turn it off before it ends).

Chase has been said to have a penis. Chase has been assumed to follow the rigid trajectory of penis-bearers. Chase, for nearly everyone who knows Chase, is a "he."

I've had neither the opportunity nor the patience (though I should, admittedly, make the opportunity and patience) to involve my immediate given family in a lengthy discussion of gender imposition and gender roles and norms and the like. The small gesture I've made thus far is to never refer to my brother's kid, Chase, as my "nephew," as "he," as my brother's "son." It is always, for me, "How's Chase doing?"; "Chase is always doing something Chase ain't got no business doing"; "Chase has way too much energy for Chase's own good." It wears on the ears, one's name over and over. It jars the senses, disrupts flows. How does a name undo itself? How does a name begin to chip away at monumental edifices unnoticed by others? Can it?

I want to see Chase in all of Chase's complexity and illegibility. *Chase* holds all that it must and everything else it cannot, while *he* rejects so, so much that Chase won't even get to sift through. How dare *he* and all his acolytes—*him, his, son, boy*—coercively and pre-emptively foreclose the flourishing of Chase's subjectivity, Chase's possible illegible gender, which would be beautiful; Chase's possible unnamed sexuality, which would be lively; Chase's unconcern with fitting in, which would be, in a word, Chase choosing to live in the all of Chase's self. Chase's purported *he* is inelegantly unable to hold *her*, to hold *they*. The only ethical and compassionate encounter I can have with Chase is perhaps one that urges Chase's unknowability. Unknown, Chase can embody the dopest of genders and the illest of comportments Chase dares to imagine. And they'll ask how, they'll wonder in awe, asking *Sugar, sugar, how'd you get so fly?*

In short, I am in an admittedly small way (though small ways can be the biggest ways) refusing to throw my brother's kid into a boat with tigers and hounds ready to devour Chase's femininity, Chase's nonnormative bodily movements, Chase's openness. I will not toss Chase into a caste waiting to beat Chase, proverbially and literally, into rigidity. But it has already started, as it always does. Even before Chase gasped air in this world Chase was trapped and will, to the extent that Chase can or wishes to, or knows Chase can, spend a lifetime trying to escape and work that trap.

Well, Chase, you joyful mischievous kid, you: here's a tiny raft if you ever want a way out. Chase, my brother's kid. There are other ways to be.

"The key is training your ear not to mind hearing a person's name over and over again. You must learn to take cover in grammatical cul-de-sacs, relax into an orgy of specificity. You must learn to tolerate an instance beyond the Two, precisely at the moment of attempting to represent a partnership—a nuptial, even."

— Maggie Nelson, *The Argonauts*

November 20, 2017

Today marks another Transgender Day of Remembrance (TDOR). TDOR began in November of 1998, growing out of Gwendolyn Ann Smith's Boston-based campaign to mourn and politicize the murder of Black trans woman Rita Hester. This was a culmination—is an ongoing culmination—of efforts that have been in place since the early 1990s, like the advocacy of Nancy Nangeroni, founder of the Boston chapter of The Transexual Menace, and Riki Anne Wilchins, founder of the Boston-based Gender Public Advocacy Coalition (GenderPAC), who held vigils for murdered trans people in Boston and demanded investigations for unsolved murders while refusing to take the mess of local media outlets who constantly misgendered slain victims.

This year, 2017, has been the deadliest year on record for trans people worldwide. In the twelve months from October 1, 2016, to September 30, 2017, according to the Transgender Murder Monitoring Project, 325 trans, nonbinary, or gender-variant people were murdered, Brazil leading the way with over 170 murders.

TDOR caps off Transgender Awareness Week and often includes, in addition to public mourning—which is a coalitional means by which the marginalized assert that their lives are indeed lives and hence grievable—the recitation of the names of those slain by transantagonistic violence that year, a roll call overwhelmingly populated with Black and Brown trans women. What I find immensely powerful too, though, is the adaptation, not the obfuscation, of this practice to include remembrance and celebration of trans lives that are still being lived, celebration of the resilience and refusal of abjection of trans people still here. This epitomizes the oft-rephrased Mother Jones quote to remember the dead and fight like hell for the living. The growing shift from Transgender Day of Remembrance to Transgender Day of *Resilience* necessarily dismantles the stilted images of deathbound trans identity and unapologetically moves toward a celebration of trans life.

It is imperative, at least for me and the folks with whom I seek to be in coalition, that we note very keenly what Nat Raha in all her radical trans feminist glory posted on her Facebook for TDOR: TDOR is and must be "about racialised, predominantly anti-black transphobic, femmephobic & whorephobic violence." The murder of trans people cannot be extricated from the anti-Blackness present in the murder of Black trans women or the pathologization and criminalization of sex workers or transmisogyny. Trans justice and any purportedly radical beat you wanna bounce to, if it is to be deserving of the name "radical," must heed the acumen provided by those mobilizing around the liberatory forces and identities of Blackness, transness, and feminism.

"We have to remember against modes of remembering that forget how transgender and Trans Day Of Remembrance is grounded in the materialities of anti-black racism and Black resistance. We also have to actively forget ways of seeing and remembering ourselves and communities as nothing: we have to practice being as an active attempt to forget what we look like through Western eyes."

— CeCe McDonald, Kai M. Green, and Treva C. Ellison, "An Introduction: When Remembering Forgets, What Forgetting Remembers"

December 4, 2017

Teaching one of my Feminist Essays classes last spring, in our brief section on masculinity and (male) feminism (the "male" always an unstable term subject to interrogation and undoing), I placed myself in one of the small groups. There were four groups and only three male students, so I inserted myself into the remaining group to even out the numbers. One of my students, a Dominican woman from Brooklyn, asked about how I grapple with masculinity, how I understand myself in relation to it. I shared with her and the three other women in the group something with which I still grapple: that I do not want to be a man. I don't want all the violent archives that come with being a man—though rejecting these archives is an impossible task to be sure, and one I do not take lightly, as if I can jettison the privileges accorded to me on the grounds of how my body is understood.

Yeah, I know, I fit almost all the typical criteria of "being a man." At least the criteria that have been consolidated in and on the body. But that is not what we mean, entirely, by *being a man*. I, too, share the *divine* (and, being viciously atheist, I do not use this term lightly) wisdom of the Combahee River Collective's (CRC) Black Feminist Statement; I, too, "have a great deal of criticism and loathing for what men have been socialized to be in this society: what they support, how they act, and how they oppress. But we do not have the misguided notion that it is *their maleness, per se—i.e., their biological maleness—* that makes them what they are."[3] (Note that we can and should query what is even meant by "biological maleness," instead of treating it as a self-evident term.) Being a man comes with much, much more than simply having the biological goods, as it were. It is an entire world, an inhabitation, that necessitates a violent position toward the feminine, toward gendered deviancy, toward emotion and value, care, assessment, relations and relationships, life. The CRC has a radical outlook with respect to gender essentialism and affirms the possibility of refusing that which one is purportedly biologically determined to be. We become men, and, consequently, we can, and must, unbecome the men we were told we have to be.

So when I say that I have a disdain for being a man, that I don't want to be a man, I am saying that I seek to jettison that archive of socialization. I don't want all the shit that I'm coerced to be. The real challenge, and it's a terrifying one, is to take serious steps toward ripping the man from myself and, as it were, manning *down*. I don't want to be a man because I don't want to do what it requires of me. Revoke my pass. I welcome it. That will at least give me more room to exist.

"Ten responses to the phrase 'Man up': 1. Fuck you."
— Guante, "Ten Responses to the Phrase 'Man Up'"

December 20, 2017

Fuck white cis supremacist capitalist heteropatriarchy. I'm going underground, where stalactites midwife jagged edges and our subterranean respite is a covert prepping for a more overt action. (Thank you, Ralph.)

January 12, 2018

My partner and I went to the Baltimore Aquarium after stopping inside a massive Barnes & Noble where you know I had to get some books. While the aquarium as a whole was dope, especially its jellyfish exhibit, I was struck by a sign for a nonhuman animal that wasn't even present: the mudskipper. Depicting an image of the less-than-attractive creature, the sign read: "Mudskippers 'walk,' jump, and climb across mudflats on agile fins and breathe air through wet skin." A versatile creature, the mudskipper, to me, strikes me as thoroughly, awesomely trans.

They move in different ways, refusing the strictures of how they would be expected to work their bodies. Walk if you wish, swim when you'd like, jump without legs, climb and scale when it interests you. Transverse movement; movement of the otherwise, move like you ain't got no business moving. The mudskipper makes me hope for some evolutionary shift that will someday engender this otherwise for us. But who has that kind of time? For now, we have the mudskipper, able to store water in its gills and be aquatic while terrestrial. It breathes by other means because breath is a precarious thing, so you'd better find as many unanticipated ways to sustain your life as possible. If they expect you to run by swimming away, jump instead, because they can't look up that high. If they expect you to jump, suspended temporarily while they wait for your descent, climb the tree or the wall or the log; they won't expect that either. If they expect you to remain bound to land, dip into the aquatic terrain the depths of which we cannot know. And if they expect all of that, burrow underground, where you store your emergent kin in a subterranean bastion of darkness that prepares you for other ways of living.

This is the mudskipper, my nonhuman animal homie. We are both hoping for different kinds of breath, various forms of motion, versatile plans of escape. I may not have caught up yet, but I'm on my way. Wait for me, mudskipper, I'm making my way there.

January 27, 2018

With the new semester approaching rapidly I've been immersed in the pungent smog of academic discourse. That is no diss, I assure you; it is a discourse that I love, and one I might be forced to mimic here out of the sheer need for precision, for getting the language out right. This is a method of thought. If I repeat myself it is only because I'm trying to get the language, the thoughts, out precisely. I'm trying to get these ideas of self-determination and abolition out as precisely as I can. I don't care much if they're wrong. Even though I know for some it means everything.

Indeed, if one is to do the work of claiming the lovingly tortuous beast of Blackness, one is also claiming the radicality of gender self-determination. Centering Black radicalism, its animating Black feminism, is, as Eric A. Stanley writes, "to already be inside trans politics."[4] Fugitive Blackness is all about that radical futurity, that radically open secret of nonnormative sociality. In a way, Blackness refuses to succumb to the legibility of the here, the before, the what should or will happen. Because of this, and because Blackness troubles gender, gender self-determination is a Black practice—it is a social praxis in subversion of pragmatics on the grounds that pragmatics uses the situation and logics at hand (which is to say hegemonic, normative tools) to think through doing life differently. In refusing, gender self-determination "struggles to make freedom flourish through a radical trans politics. Not only a defensive posture, it builds in the name of the undercommons a world beyond the world," a worldliness that will not go away and, while remaining here, will not heed the world's rules. Gender self-determination is intimate with the Black sociality of the undercommons, thinking gendered life in and as "the excesses of gendered life" and understanding gender-troubling Blackness as the "moment of radical possibility."

When advancing self-determination, we must understand it as distinct from what is *determined*. It is an open self-determination, one that, to the extent that the hegemonic process of gendering is the violent giving and imposition of an ontology, effectively *ungenders*, insofar as determining one's own gender (not, of course, without acknowledging the troublesome impossibility of an unfettered "choice") is to refuse its antithesis, gendering from without. Too, it must be noted that gender self-determination inherently reconditions how "self" is understood, since, rather than being neoliberal praise of individualistic freedom to choose whatever one wishes, self-determination as a constant liberatory struggle at the site of those "gender skirmishes on the edges" is necessarily entwined with all other revolutionary struggles. The revolutionary politics of gender self-determination is also, always, to advance self-determination via other identity vectors on the grounds that the "revolutionary politics of self-determination must also be about recognizing and challenging systems of white supremacist capitalism and neocolonialism."[5] Gender self-determination challenges all structures of domination because gender pervades all of them, therefore any radical politics must include a radical, self-determining gender politics.

Because abolition has, effectively, no precedent (no, not even 1865 in the United States) yet is still a term of identification and a performative aim, abolition as affixed to gender is a way to refuse the hold of our given gendered ontology. Externally imposed genders that pre-cede one's identification and foreclose one's refusal of identification are a captivity demanding servility to its laws. Gender abolition's self-determination is apparent when we understand that gender abolition is gender that is not (yet here), it is gender ungendered, it is gender in the undercommons, it is gender for those who refuse gender. In the beyond of this refusal is "the abolition of a society *that could have* prisons, that could have slavery, that could have the wage, and there-fore *not abolition as the elimination of anything but abolition as the founding of a new society.*"[6]

We are hearing, here, abolition as a mode of being against social relations invested and investing in promises of sovereignty and self-possession. This goal of abolition is not a form of self-possession "that could have" (including the capacity to eliminate anything); rather, in its unconditional vulnerability to not simply the relations of material or symbolic possession but also the very capacity to possess anything, it can be understood as a mode of being with and in dispossession.

February 20, 2018

Danny, my beloved comrade and intellectual sparring partner, sent me a text as I sat on campus reading.

> So. . . . I've been thinking through questions of identity a lot—my per-sonal identity. Not sure I've really told anyone this before but I don't feel like /anything/—I feel like I can identify /with/ anything when I want to, but not "as." I am a male—and happy to be one, I like my body—but I don't feel like a male, nor do I feel like a female. I am the grand majority of time sexually attracted to men—but I don't feel like a homosexual, or a heterosexual, or a bisexual. . . . I am a human, and this may seem strange, but I don't feel like a human, or an animal,

or a god. I'm not properly a theist or an atheist or an agnostic. Even career-wise, I feel like I /could be/ anything if I simply desired to be and followed the necessary path. All it would take is desire—the desire to identify as something at a moment, but otherwise unconcerned. Basically I seem to identify most /with/ "nothing" and/or balance (which could be the midpoint of everything and nothing, but who wants to get philosophical?). [We do, my friend! We always do ☺] That's why you made me so happy the one day when you said I seemed parentless like I walked out of the sea haha. Because what the hell, where did I come from anyway? I belong nowhere and everywhere. Identity has always infuriated me as a concept haha

I feel like my response to "how do you identify" would be properly "as I wish" lol

I responded to him from a place of giddiness, love, rapport, and understanding:

Okay, so your text got ME thinking, though I've been thinking about these things for a while. First, the personal: So I always hesitate to answer, and feel like a liar, when I'm asked if I'm "straight." While I've almost exclusively been romantically and sexually attracted to (what I assume are) cis women, I have also been romantically involved with a sexually queer woman and a genderqueer person who identified as female (but not "woman"). Too, because of my commitment to and knowledge of transgender studies, I take issue with presuming myself heterosexual, largely because I adhere to the trans axiom that no one's gender can be assumed ahead of itself (the refusal to exist ahead of oneself, a kind of radical existentialism). Heterosexuality, to me, (1) is predicated on the assumption of a gender binary, and (2) erases the possibility of the transness, as it were, of, say, someone whom I may find attractive, who might be a trans woman. Are cis men who may find a trans woman attractive properly "straight" in that scenario?

So I've taken to doing two things: being more and more comfortable with understanding myself as queer—in the capacious sense, or rather in a Black queer feminist sense the likes of, say, Cathy Cohen, who understands queer as a subversive relation to power deployed through various indices of gender in particular. (I've even told Kate [my partner] that queer much better describes me, and she was thoroughly okay with and understanding of that.) As well, I've taken to being very okay with being addressed with the gender-nonbinary pronoun "they/them."

Second, the academic: I think I told you that my Caputo [in reference to John D. Caputo, Danny's intellectual love] is a Black studies scholar named Fred Moten. He is my everything. For him, he's understanding Blackness as NOT tied to the epidermal but as what he calls "fugitivity." There's this awesome quote he has in his new book that is particularly relevant for what you said: "Indeed, our resistant, relentlessly impossible object is subjectless predication, subjectless escape, escape from subjection, in and through the paralegal flaw that animates and exhausts the language of ontology. Constant escape is an ode to impurity, an obliteration of the last word. We remain to insist upon this errant, interstitial insistence." Now that shit is beautiful! But yes, this pursuit of subjectlessness, escape from subjection, which is what ontology is—a normative metaphysical violence, one might say. What you seem to be yearning for is, again citing Moten, a "paraontology." What you seem to be yearning for is a fugitive escape that is itself motivated by an aim for subjectless predication, life in the interstitial. And this is why we are comrades, family: we want to be fugitives together.

It sounds like Danny is trying to get to what has been deemed "flesh," as distinct from the rigidity of the body. The body's metaphysical weight constricts Danny, and he wants out; his "as I wish" might index a self-determinative, transed, excessive desire for radical liberation. Our goal, if we are to get outta all this mess, is to sub out the overbearing structuring regime of metaphysics—the omni-sovereign force that delimits our horizon—to instead bring in our ringer: *metaphysique*. If our existing metaphysic aims only to contain us, something new might be possible in a metaphysique, a way to contort our bodies—which are hemmed in by metaphysical dictates—outside of themselves toward the flesh, that thing we must love hard, that thing that exceeds the various apparatuses of capture. Our metaphysique, flexing and bending in ways they can't anticipate, lean and mean with excessive uncapturability, is the fleshy surplus of the body that ushers us into another way to exist in the world. The metaphysique could be a world unto itself, a livable grace that can't be hedged.

Could it be that a metaphysique, in its etymological allusion to being meta-, beyond, the dictates of the physical, is what happens to a body when it shrouds itself in and steps its way through the rules of a goon? Could it be that when we escape in fugitive flight we slough off the baggage of our body and the laws of the world and begin to fashion a subjectivity on the run from the *physical* into the *metaphysiqual*?

Danny replied to my text immediately, saying, "Omg you made me cry lol. . . . In the best way."

And that is where Danny and I are. Yearning for subjectless subjectivity.

"I don't want to be a lady."

— Arya Stark, *Game of Thrones*

April 8, 2018

I was asked by a dear friend of mine—an invaluable interlocutor who happens to be, of all things, primarily a chemist—how I understood violence. I do not recall the context of our discussion, as it was some weeks ago and I have of late been preoccupied with intellectual insecurities, bouts of immense lethargy, and hours of cartoon binge-watching (hence the lull in entries). But when he asked me about violence, how I understood it, where I stood in relation to violence or nonviolence (though he did not put it in such dichotomous terms), my answer, I know, was insufficient. I've long relied upon my distance from physical violence to delay any prolonged meditation on the subject. And, on reflection, the aforementioned distance from physical violence is a lie; I am never distanced from it. Nevertheless, my perception that I have lived a somewhat calm life has given me the illusion that violence does not concern me and mine.

I've since done some thinking. As a child of Southwest Philly and an adolescent of a borough not too far from it—and, too, as the literal child of a father who, through most of his teenage years into his late twenties, was affiliated with Philly's Junior Black Mafia and has been shot three times—violence has always been a familiar specter. From my mother's near-serious injury in a car accident caused by an ex-boyfriend attempting to pull her from the vehicle after punching her, to a brother whom I've seen scrap on multiple occasions (and, reader, he did not always win), spectacular iterations of violence have punctuated my years. Too, the violence of de jure segregation, the violence of poverty, the violence of racialized optics, the violence of gendered assault and assumptions all seeped into too-close proximity to me. So I can only in arrogant ignorance claim that violence has not visited my life. It has, in fact, constituted it.

One might think, as my friend certainly did, that I would be no stranger to affirmative assessments of violence. But I want to understand my relation to it as more complex than that. I must. The various ways in which my life has been constituted by violence, I want to believe, necessitate a kind of responsibility—or a plea, really, an existential prayer—to refuse the proliferation of violence. You see, I want to viscerally practice the mode of thought that "it should still be possible to claim that a certain crucial breakage can take place between the violence by which we are formed and the violence by which we conduct ourselves once formed."[7] The difficult thing to conceptualize is what that "crucial breakage" might mean in the face of a world that seeks to eradicate so many of us. I know the colloquialism and I know the stats; I know that being mired in a cauldron textured by various kinds of violence structures one's reality as fundamentally violent, which structures one's horizon of possibility for life and living. This I get, but I yearn for the mitigation of violence. My very subjectivity is the product of an imposed template, given from without, which has made me me. That is a violence of ontological proportions. The violence of the norms that constitute us—which is only to say that I am me largely because I was told what the components of "me" are supposed to be, a decision I have had much less influence over than I'd like—is a fundamental slight. What are we to do with this?

I am rambling, perhaps, and you are wondering what this has to do with Blackness, with queerness, with transness. All and nothing; a little and a lot. The attempt of liberationists to extricate the marginalized from categorical impositions is, at base, a praxis of nonviolence. But I want to distance this, so very slightly, from a King, Jr.–esque understanding of nonviolent direct action (don't forget that *direct action*, as so many neoliberal folks do). *This* nonviolence is in the service, first and foremost, of abolishing the violence that betides us at the level of the *sociogenic*: the ways in which we come to exist in and through sociality. What that means is this nonviolence is uninterested in your feel-good notions of turning the other cheek. This nonviolence might, and I think does and should, believe, as Andrea Gibson has poetically inscribed, that "there is such a thing as a nonviolent fist."[8] This nonviolence might sock you in the face because it wants so fiercely to shut down the proliferation of violence. It might take another way, an otherwise way, an illegible way, to get there. An ethics begotten by fugitivity attends to how we intentionally think about our effects in the world, rendering us not immobile but much more cognizant of how we inhabit the world and how our inhabitation affects other forms of life. Being bred in and through violence must necessitate that we refuse to breed others in and through violence.

Follow me: perhaps there is something to say about how the way in which Blackness, queerness, transness unsuture what purports to be cohesive and impenetrable is itself a fundamentally ethical gesture. See, if there is necessarily a violence to having one's identity imposed from without, then fracturing those impositions might be an undoing of that violence. Persistently interrupting and undermining the violence of nonconsensually constructing my horizon of possibility (who I'm permitted to be) can maybe serve as a nonviolent praxis. And that, my friends, is a Black queer and trans praxis.

"How fragile and contingent is 'ordinary,' unviolated existence."

—— Bruce B. Lawrence and Aisha Karim, *On Violence*

April 24, 2018

At a conference I recently attended, a conference on transforming queerness, I used, like I've done about a dozen times before, a gender-neutral bathroom. The what-I-assumed-were-your-traditional "Men" or "Women" signs were covered by a white sheet of paper on which was written, "This bathroom is for everyone." I smiled because I felt the love, the openness, the ethical commitment to ensuring the proliferative safety of proliferative genders. This was radical love.

Weeks after this conference I was asked about trans people and bathrooms. It was a genuine question, one I understood as inviting insight for later use, perhaps when speaking with someone who was less understanding and, as one might say, less trans-friendly. So I want to further meditate on the "bathroom debate," since it converges with the trans-inclusivity and radical world-alteration so palpable at the Audre Lorde Project.

The bathroom debate makes it plain that the public toilet is a fertile political site because it is a unique space in which many social regimes converge: regulation of the gender/sex binary, disciplining of disability, regulation of bodies of Color, and, broadly speaking, dictation of who is welcomed in public space. Gaining the most steam with North Carolina's House Bill 2 (HB2), anti-trans policies concerned with the site of the public restroom speak largely to safety. The discourse often goes, "We need to stop these predatory men in dresses from preying on our daughters, wives, and mothers." The crux of the backlash to more inclusive restrooms is the sanctity of (white) cis womanhood. As Kathi Weeks observes, rhetoric surrounding the public toilet and transgender access to it in fact "trivializes what remains a pervasive social problem that obviously occurs more often in households than in public toilets and ignores other instances of violence, including the well-documented instances of violence to which transgender people have been subjected and the violence done to people around the world."[9] In other words, here's the deal: the conservative, right-wing mania about trans women gaining access to women's bathrooms to sexually harass or terrorize cis women is bullshit because the overwhelming majority of the violence done to women, sexual and non-sexual, occurs in the home at the hands of cis men, and trans women are far more likely to be the ones harassed. The fantasy of the trans predator is one conjured by the dominant narrative of how we understand a masculine propensity for violence, and is an indication of our inability to imagine trans women as women who are subject to many of the same kinds of sexual and gendered vulnerabilities as the very women folks are railing about.

The fixation on safety, while surely we want a safer world for women who have a history of being subject to gendered violence, is disingenuous and obscures the pervasiveness of violence against queer, trans, and femme people, *overwhelmingly committed by cis men*, that occurs outside the politically charged space of the public restroom. Ain't none of y'all talking about how dudes are beating their wives; about how you chastise your daughters for breaching the narrow-ass confines of demure, "proper" femininity; about pervasive rape culture, intimate partner violence, street harassment, stalking. Similar to the way anti-choice proponents tout how "pro-life" they are yet have little to say about—and often instantiate policies that disallow—the thriving continuation of that life once outside the womb, so too anti-trans rabble-rousers scream about cis women's safety in locker rooms and bathrooms but are tellingly silent about what happens to them once they leave these places. The concern over cis women's safety coming from supporters of anti-trans legislation is a ruse, because rather than being about violence against non-masculine-gendered subjects, in which case we would be having much longer and broader conversations, it is about the refusal to take seriously trans women's claims to womanhood. (Notice, too, how this is almost exclusively a conversation about trans women, not trans men, as the latter would not allow for the discussion to be sensationalized and paternalistically concern the safety of "our women.")

It's imperative to note, too, the spectral presence of Blackness. Only a few decades ago the public bathroom was a site of gender being collapsed and disintegrated when affixed to Blackness—that is, during Jim and Jane Crow one saw only three signs, not the four that one might (still problematically) expect: "Women," "Men," and "Colored." So anti-trans lawfare must always be understood as conversant with the history of racial slavery and the criminalization of nonnormative genders. The presumptively sexed subject, needing always to be a "properly" sexed subject, is, too, a racialized subject—at least in the symbolic imaginary of sex and gender—and illuminates how "Black and/or indigenous peoples have always figured as sexual and gender outlaws to be disciplined and punished."[10] If we also consider the function of the birth certificate as the presumed locus of authorized documentary "truth" regarding one's gender identity, we see how this, too, is marked by the troublesome history of racialization. (Not to mention that to argue that the designation on the birth certificate arbitrates "real" biological sex then makes sex a matter of documentation, divorced entirely from the body.) Y'all show your racist and xenophobic colors when you make recourse to documentation as the be-all and end-all, because the rhetoric strongly weaves anti-trans beliefs into anti-immigrant and anti-Black sentiments. Efforts to deny birth certificates to children of undocumented parents, attempts to use immigrants' undocumented status as grounds for their harassment and expulsion, and the suspect ways folks attempted to discredit former president Obama's claim to the presidency (which is to say, his racial transgression of the highest seat in the executive branch) by demanding his birth certificate speak to the racialized history of documentation.

It's evident that the public toilet indexes such torturous histories of racial segregation, and, I hope, it becomes clearer how the discourse surrounding anti-trans laws like HB2 is *primarily* about maintaining the regulative regimes that discipline raced, sexed, classed, and dis/abled bodies. I'll put it another way: all this talk about bathrooms registers how anxious we so often are about "those people" entering into spaces predicated on normative exclusions (the brouhaha over women's rooms being established to accommodate women's entrance into the [paid] workforce, the fear of gay men using public bathrooms during the AIDS crisis, hissy fits over making bathrooms more accessible to folks with disabilities, etc.). The insurrectionary politics that is Black and trans and queer and feminist is, at base, a "politics [that] rest[s] on affirmations that transformation is possible, that our fates are not sealed at birth, that borders, prison walls, and other regulatory barriers can be unmade, and that biology is not destiny."[11]

"By claiming that sex is 'biological sex,' the letter [on the birth certificate, M or F] seems to assert that sex is equal to genital shape. But note that this is not the advancement of a simple materialism that would conflate a person's sex with that person's genitals. The genitals to which it refers are the genitals of a newborn, genitals that may have no relation at all to one's current physical body. This is an understanding of 'biological' that is almost entirely dematerialized from the phenomenology of the body, either in its appearance from the outside or in its feeling from the inside."

— Gayle Salamon, *The Life and Death of Latisha King: A Critical Phenomenology of Transphobia*

May 25, 2018

These journal entries have allowed me to dare in my writing. Their privacy, so to speak, while made public to you, reader, is nevertheless a secretive and submerged practice of getting things out without subjecting them to the constraints of public discursive space. The genre of the journal entry enables me to convey unruly rules as a discursive space in which to practice another kind of life. This writing is both to exercise and to exorcise: to make a constant practice of the working of grammars that trans politics is continually perfecting, and to exorcise the poisonous constraints from the language we use to push ourselves into an existence. Writing the journal entries has been a practice in fugitivity, no doubt: I have not, I hope, written as if I were attempting to be something that already has a place in this world, governed by various logics; I have written, perhaps, as something trying to emerge from the muck of the submerged.

"So write. . . . Not like a girl. Not like a boy. Write like a motherfucker."

— Cheryl Strayed, *Tiny Beautiful Things:*
Advice on Love and Life from Dear Sugar

Three Theses

*Black/Feminist/Queer**

T he following theses, at some length, are musings on what I
see as the fugitive spirit, if you will, of Blackness, feminism,
and queerness. They are claims, radically open claims, that
attempt to think about recalibrated ways of being. In their openness,
they undergo perpetual revision; they constantly exceed themselves as
definitive claims. And I am scared (so, so scared) to say these things,
a fright that I've long tried to mitigate but cannot. But as my theses,
they are pleas for a way to be otherwise. They are pleas for life other
than what it has come to be. Fugitive life.

I.

But what is most important is that blackness itself, insofar
as it stands in for the inadequacy of mechanistic explana-
tion . . . is a physicality that is indexed to something more

* Part of this essay was originally published on *RaceBaitR* under the title
"Ain't Never Scared: The Necessity of Learning from Black Feminist Refusal,"
on August 14, 2017.

than the "merely" physical. . . . But what is the materiality and physicality of blackness? I would tend to agree with both Kant and Du Bois that simple description doesn't come close to getting at that animaterial, metaphysical thing in itself that exceeds itself

— Fred Moten, "Taste Dissonance Flavor Escape:
Preface for a Solo by Miles Davis"

The above epigraph from Moten's "Taste Dissonance Flavor Escape" has enraptured me since I read it as a second-year PhD student. What would it mean for Blackness to exceed materiality and physicality and to fail to be captured by simple description? (I've noticed also, on second read, that in the article the sentence is missing a period; it exceeds the literal periodization of the sentence, unable to be contained or closed, always radically open.) What would it mean to take this seriously as another kind of Black life? If Blackness is the name for animateriality, or the thing that animates the material, its fugitive thinking and disobedience, what does this force us, often against the visceral commitments and desires and affective ties we have, to do? How would the world and our relationship with it and its inhabitants change if Blackness named something else? I want to suggest that Blackness is open (and always opening); Blackness, too, is and holds and is held by the queer, the feminist planning, the trans. Linking these nodes of Blackness, and the Blackness that is the node of each of these, is the itch to escape, to shift and become otherwise, to side-eye the normative. To live by unruly goon rules. To burrow into and out of this fugitivity is to welcome the deviant and the deviance that beckons us all in subversion of propriety. Answer this call, and keep answering it. It exceeds itself as a category; Blackness, indeed, exceeds categorization, making it somethin' else ("You are somethin' else," my familial kinfolk used to—and still—say around the block, knowing that someone was and was not who they should be). Blackness stems from its escapeful somethin' else–ness.

So it seems safe to say that the forthcoming theses will disturb. But this is the work of Blackness. The forthcoming theses cannot help but vitiate notions of purity. But, again, this is the work of Blackness. I've been thinking fearfully about ideas that trouble me and no doubt have troubled colleagues and friends—and I have the strained relationships and lost friendships to show for it—for myriad reasons, chief among which is, I think, a relentless hold on the legible, the known, the comforting, the norm. Their discomfort signals to me something profound. To be sure, touting my intellectual "haters" is no means of garnering intellectual clout. I am sure I have not been the most pleasant or convincing, my disposition not always entirely collegial. But this is the onset of a thesis that addresses the poignant question of what it might mean to refuse exclusion as a radical coalitional praxis.

To give the name "Blackness" to the force of fugitivity, subversion, and reaching constantly for the nonnormative highlights Blackness's refusal of closure and coherence, of the pure. Indeed, "what is inadequate to blackness is already given ontologies," ergo Blackness must be thought, problematically (in that it causes a problem), before/now/futuristically "as a destabilizing force against the project of racial purity, of aesthetic distinction."[1] Self-determination is an inherency of Blackness, unhappy with what it has been given as its character, yearning for some illegibility to exude as a valid identity for itself. It is a globalized openness and a radical, and no doubt terrifying, inclusiveness. It is always acknowledging the radical tradition's insistence on the always tentativeness of theorizing freedom; it resides in the penchant for escape, the subversion of normative regimes, the deregulation of regulation, the openness to undoing, the dwelling with deviancy, the quotidian practice of refusal, the anoriginary transitive lawlessness, the transverse boogeydown sidestep, the undercommon relation to power, the nonbinaristic multitude. This is the Blackness animating our racial and gendered onslaught, neither melanin nor an "unquestioning fidelity to the tribe," but an impossible and improvisational choice amid choicelessness; a disruptive daringness, the *imaginative, modern, out-of-the-house, outlawed, unpolicing, uncontained, and uncontainable*.[2] That's what I'm talking about.

The very move to begin the task of writing about, or rather with, Blackness is always spectrally haunted by an upheaval. Blackness, if I am to claim anything about it, is never stable, always moving artfully in a submerged and subverting escape. Exhausting because it is inexhaustible, it overflows enframement. It refuses chillness and marks the moment when even turnt gets turnt up.

> So what is blackness . . . ? That's a good question. The exact same one the immortal French author Jean Genet posed after being asked by an actor to write a play featuring an all-black cast, when he mused not only "What exactly is a black?" but added the even more fundamental inquiry, "First of all, what is his [sic] color?"

What if we strap Blackness to a multilevel fugitive spirit that produces unexpected effects that bear on sociality and troublesomely implodes the Law by laughing at and making laughable ("Tell the coppers 'hahahaha'. . . .") the highest, perhaps most divine terrestrial instantiation of the nation's claim to authoritative Law? Genet asks what is the color of "the Black" because his fundamental attempt is to understand Blackness, to locate it, as something that exceeds physicality. It is, in fact, something closer to a posture, a penchant, a consciousness, a disposition. Paul Beatty, from whose novel *The Sellout* the above quote is taken, quite frankly scares us in his allusion to this elsewhere. Indeed, he scares me—his fearlessness, his unapologetic openness and absurdity. His lack of piety, on his account, allows for an ultimate transgression that opens up the radical possibility of something, terrifyingly, quite different. This is a radical, risky openness, and the openness of possibility in all its various shades—literal and not—is where it happens.

A colleague of mine—an epidermally white man who works in and through Black studies, and who thinks about the excessive present of abolition—engaged me, as usual, in rich conversation about Blackness. His reluctance to distinguish Blackness from people deemed epidermally Black was palpable, and his concerns sensible. As I attempted to relay my understanding of Blackness as fugitivity, he concurred only until one reaches the threshold of those instances when skin read as Black indeed matters, and is perhaps the only thing that matters. "If you and I both get stopped by the cops," he said, "we have very different experiences despite our similar political and ideological views." I would absolutely concede this point. "Now, I'd definitely—because of the work that I do—feel super-conflicted about it and understand how my whiteness largely protects me from the white supremacist violence of the law," he continued, "but nevertheless my skin is a shield, no matter how much I—and I do—struggle."

All I could muster in the midst of his genuinely conveyed reserve was, "Perhaps, though, that struggle, that confliction, that muddying of the luminosity of your whiteness—which is to say, that Blackening of yourself—*is* a type of Blackness." And here is when he gave the most profound, genuine pause. In that moment of sociality I was urging the revising and correcting of "Blackness" to refer to a fugitive movement and interrogative posture. Here I am suggesting an understanding—on the insurrectionary heels of John Brown, or following the risky, revolutionary dwelling in fugitive spirit of Marilyn Buck—that resonates with and takes deeply, contentiously seriously what Fred Moten has called "blackness's distinction from a specific set of things called black."[3] My colleague, I think, emerges not as a white ally or mere "woke" white dude; his political identity—which is to say, recalibrated, *identity as such*—affirms, to quote Moten again, that *everyone whom blackness claims, which is to say everyone, can claim blackness.* The work my colleague does is Black radical work, a work that inaugurates a substantive vector of his subjectivity. To "claim" Blackness, a claiming that gives freely, is to do its work.

Operative here is a recalibration of the logic to one where Blackness is gotten at via alliance and contagion, affiliation and attainment, proximity and capacity. This is a tapping into Blackness's queerness, if we understand queerness as not simply a sexual desire but a radical disruption of gender norms; this is Blackness's otherwise identification located in the interstices, frictional relations, and rebellious communing with those we are not supposed to commune with. In other words, Blackness, reconceptualized in this way, is a way of relating otherwise that is not predicated on blood quantum or declarations of law. Blackness names one of the many fugitive ways we effectively recompose subjectivities in the name of liberation.

This same colleague noted, too, on another occasion, that to do the work to which he surely commits himself, to be 'bout that life of Blackness, is to risk. Perhaps that is one way that Blackness can look: being a threat to hegemonic power to the extent that you risk your subjectivity, your life and livelihood, your cohesion. In this sense, to elaborate this through a literary parallel that would make all my English teachers happy, my colleague allows me to think Blackness-as-risk through the ever-adventurous Huckleberry Finn. We know good ol' Huck, but what we may not know is that Huck got real-Black-raw as the novel progressed. I am being hyperbolic, surely, but I might also venture to say that I am not. This is the difficult, scary work I cannot help but do. As Huck contemplates sending the letter he wrote to Miss Watson informing her of the whereabouts of her "runaway nigger," Jim, Huck says:

> I was a-trembling, because I'd got to decide, forever, betwixt two things, and I knowed it. I studied a minute, sort of holding my breath, and then says to myself:
> "All right, then, I'll *go* to hell"—and tore it [the letter] up.

It was awful thoughts and awful words, but they was said. And I let them stay said; and never thought no more about reforming. I shoved the whole thing out of my head, and said I would take up wickedness again, which was in my line, being brung up to it, and the other warn't. And for a starter I would go to work and steal Jim out of slavery again; and if I could think up anything worse, I would do that, too; because as long as I was in, and in for good, I might as well go the whole hog.

Toward the end of the novel, Huck runs into his pal Tom Sawyer and reveals his fugitive adventures (after convincing Tom that he is not a ghost):

"All right; but wait a minute. There's one more thing—a thing that *nobody* don't know but me. And that is, there's a nigger here that I'm a-trying to steal out of slavery, and his name is *Jim*—old Miss Watson's Jim."

He says:

"What! Why, Jim is—"

He stopped and went to studying. I says:

"*I* know what you'll say. You'll say it's dirty, low-down business; but what if it is? *I'm* low down; and I'm a-going to steal him, and I want you keep mum and not let on. Will you?"

His eye lit up, and he says:

"I'll *help* you steal him!"

Well, I let go all holts then, like I was shot. It was the most astonishing speech I ever heard—and I'm bound to say Tom Sawyer fell considerable in my estimation. Only I couldn't believe it. Tom Sawyer a *nigger-stealer*!

I want to posit the possibility of Huck and Tom, in these moments, indexing and mobilizing around and in and with Blackness. This Blackness is what concerns me, this affiliative deviancy, this thing

Huck calls "*go[ing]* to hell," or "no more . . . reforming," or "the whole hog" of "wickedness," or finally being and becoming a "*nigger-stealer.*" Stealing stolen life so it can steal more of itself, risking eternal damnation for the prosperity of the fugitive's fugitivity, refusing reformation, being in the business of "dirty, low-down business" is what it means to occupy the coalitional and fugitive space of Blackness. It is a disobedience to the prevailing law of enslavement. They have entered into Blackness, which is how we all, from various and disparate places and via myriad desires, come to Blackness. We must enter into it and do its bidding; we must steal and help steal, get so low-down and dirty we end up brushing shoulders with Lucifer, deviating from and flouting reformation because we just can't be fixed (and reject fixedness). Blackness resides all up over here.

So while recognizing the visceral import of the sufficiently Black surface (it was Jim, after all, who ran first), the surface and the reactions it engenders are only one dimension of the multiplicity, the robustness, of Blackness. It is the entering into Blackness, and thus the intention of doing and moving alongside Blackness, that I wish to mark as a kind of Black work. Blackness in its fugitive volatility and shifting uncertainty is marked always by an entry, which is a hieroglyphic rearrangement of content. Entering always occurs in tortuous ways, even if we are entering a room that we cannot leave. The unleavable place of the perceptions of our epidermis, perhaps, is simultaneously a place composed entirely of entries. It does not, however, end here, as we occupy a space in many textured ways; we continue to enter spaces we have already entered and been entered into. Does one sit in the chair placed in the space for them, twiddling one's thumbs, or does one begin ripping down the wallpaper, breaking the window, digging up the floorboards, pissing and shitting everywhere but the pot they put in there for you?

Of course we can wag our finger at Tom Sawyer for making a game out of Jim's freedom, and for his ultimate compensation of Jim—"forty dollars for being prisoner for [Huck and Tom] so patient," to be exact. But with enterability comes exitability, the ability to move not only toward but away from Blackness, to commit to Blackness's work or to do it tomorrow—or the next day or the next day . . .—when one has more time. Tom enters Blackness, and subsequently exits it; Jim, too, entered Blackness when he escaped, and, I contend, can exit it by refastening his chains, securing them snugly, and "Yes, suh"–ing his way through life giddy with the control of his massa. It requires work to take up the task Blackness calls us to do. In the work is where Blackness happens.

What I am proposing is a perpetually interrogative and adaptable dimension within political activism, consistently reminding us to question the limits of our political penchants and identifications— namely, who are our kinfolk and whose livelihood do we seek to validate—when doing Blackness. The simple profundity of this last point cannot be overstated: loosely, sure, we "are" Black as a matter of bestowed measurements of melanin; additionally, too, we do our Blackness, deploy Blackness's perturbative force, doing dirt so we can, as the crass 'hood saying goes, put our niggas on. And this "we," this "our," this kinship, this family, is capacious. We let go of our norma- tive, though affective, ties. The letting go will be difficult, and it is okay if we get scared and return to the comforts of what we've always known. But this retooling demands that we reteach ourselves where we locate our kin.

> We did it. We shifted the paradigm. We rewrote the meaning of life
> with our living. And this is how we did it. We let go. And then we got
> scared and held on and then we let go again. Of everything that would
> shackle us to sameness. Of our deeply held belief that our lives could
> be measured or disconnected from anything. We let go and re-taught
> ourselves to breathe the presence of the energy that we are that cannot
> be destroyed, but only transformed and transforming everything.

Breathe deep, beloved young and frightened self, and then let go.
And you will hold on. So then let go again.[4]

II.

The fugitivity of these images lies not in their ability to sanction movement but in the creation of new possibilities for living lives that refused a regulatory regime from which they could not be removed.

— Tina Campt, "Performing Stillness"

By now we all know the significance of the date and location "Charlottesville, Virginia, August 12, 2017." At least I hope we do. Its events mark another notch in the genealogical chain of white male supremacy, one fueled by, among numerous things, terror. We are thoroughly acquainted with the various iterations of hissy fits by white men and their supremacist acolytes and sycophants. We've met this before. But this is not the lineage in which I wish to dwell. Rather, where I want to post up is the Black radical *feminist* tradition of confronting white supremacy and the Black feminist history of fugitive refusals of being "ontologically," or in one's essential being, reduced to racial and gendered abjection.

An image spangled across my Facebook timeline: that of what appeared and was assumed to be a Black woman within inches of the hooded face of a KKK member. With her face tilted slightly upward, she fixed her eyes directly at eyes too timid to announce themselves without the guise of ersatz power. This Black woman gazed back, refusing to be merely looked upon in contempt; she, in the vein of Zora Neale Hurston, chose "not to weep at the world" but instead to sharpen her "oyster knife," readying herself to lacerate the confines imposed upon her.[5] This is the legacy we must choose to inherit.

Legacies, indeed, can be and have been, and *must* be, chosen. This is a legacy of ongoing escape, of fracturing those structures that seek to coerce us into immobilized abjection, of rebellious spirit, of demanding that we neither disappear nor comply. The legacy I choose is that of the radicality of Black feminism.

What would it mean to follow, with the utmost unyielding seriousness, Hortense Spillers, who foundations her life upon a Black feminism characterized by "*subversion* itself—law breaking—[a]s an act of liberation," the "stunning idea" of rebellious *outlawry*? What would it mean to follow Toni Morrison's declaration that "there is no time for despair, no place for self-pity, no need for silence, no room for fear"? What would it mean to follow Miss Major and know that we've "been chased *but not caught*"?[6] It might mean that if we take the work of Black radical feminism seriously, allow it to pervade our sociality and saturate our lives, we will inevitably stare those hooded men and all their constituents in the face and refuse intimidation. It is the variously gendered and ungendered Black women who show us how to side-eye terror. More specifically, and, I might argue, more accurately, it is the Black feminist tradition that makes terror's various incarnations tremble. They shook, those halfway crooks.

My insistence on Black feminism—that disobedient life of loving the rupture, loving the knowledge begotten by the racial and gendered nexus of Black and woman—stems from a commitment to "ungendered" and ungendering Blackness, which deploys the disruption of white male supremacist logics by refusing terror, by reveling in those moments when captivity is exceeded. This is how the flesh goes to work when the body is curtailed by oppressive power. This is flesh exceeding violence and writing hieroglyphs on the walls that try to contain it. It is the "Nah" of Rosa Parks, an immersion in a Black feminism inherent to which is a persistent practice of refusal; it is the "We out!" of Harriet Tubman, her escape from captivity, her nonnormative gender, her suturing of life to liberatory flight laying the foundation for her liberatory will to keep runnin'; it is the "I came to slay, bitch!"

of Big Freedia, a queer and Black insurgency that troubles the norm. Y'all'ready know, it is the Black radical feminist tradition. It says that your claim to power is not recognized, and in that nonrecognition the power cannot hold. Your chains cannot fetter my flight; they rattle, clank, and break. Your templates masquerading as universal will be vitiated by my very enactment of my bad self. Go 'head with that.

And yet, I still find that the question often arises: When we got this shit coming out the woodworks, how do we continue to persist, to not feel defeated despite our most formidable efforts? Quite simply, I've learned, because we must. The claim to life on the earth we've inherited is not monopolized by the murderous limbs of hegemony—white and male supremacy, transantagonism, heteronormativity, elitism, anti-Blackness, colonial imperialism—and it extends into the generative and volatile space of the underground, the undercommons. It extends into the subversive place where the revolution radicalizes revolution, a place inhabited by folks who came together illegally and unexpectedly because they operated according to other ways of relating. We still, always, do abolition today and tomorrow as subversive intellectuals, feminist killjoys, Black radicals, "nasty women," activistic accomplices, muhfuckin' goons. We will, as Black feminists have long shown us, celebrate, because we've always, *always*, been met with imminent danger. We will celebrate—*regardless*, to creatively purloin Alice Walker—because things have always been trying to kill us. And they, once again, will fail. This is not naïveté; this is the melodious acumen of Black feminism.

Black radical feminism is the only kind of god to which I will ever feel the need to pray, as the incantatory tremors of its posture of abolishing the regimes of white, male, cis, straight, etc., etc., etc. hegemony and violence strike me as the only means by which the world's ills can be purged. Black feminism posits a radical future in which we might, hopefully, someday, live. This future resides in a Black feminist temporality, a temporal tense of anteriority noting what will have had to happen in order for the future to be realized. This Black feminist grammar is "humble and strategic, dogged, disruptive," as Tina Campt argues. But most tellingly, it is a "grammar of *possibility beyond* what will be" if the present simply plays out as it has been.[7] This grammar, concerned with the rewriting of the future through the disruption of the now, sustains Black feminist livelihood because it nourishes the possibility of living an unbounded life. We might also call this unbounded life engendered by Black feminist grammar *freedom.* And if y'all think we scared of freedom, well, you's a lie.

Y'all can't be telling lies when we got freedom dreams toward which to aspire.

We cannot mobilize around, and actualize, the radically different world in which we wish to live until we refuse the one we have been given. The refusal is where it's at; the refusal, which is to say a kind of inoculation of flesh against the supposed weightiness of normative physical and discursive structures, is the site of daring to exist otherwise. It is that Black woman leering back at the hooded eyes and asserting that all that the hood signified—a prominent, fundamental strain, one might say, of the history of this nation—could not quash her commitment to living.

Black feminism has called out the illusory weight of the Big Bad Wolf that has cloaked itself in the garb of inflated power. Black feminism has used the Wolf's government name. And what do you know, it got shook.[†]

[†] After this piece was shared across the annals of social media in excess of 1,800 times, I came across a comment that claimed that it perpetuated the ever-present myth of the "Strong Black Woman," a "controlling image," to use Patricia Hill Collins's phrase, an "entity swollen," to use Patrisse Khan-Cullors and asha bandele's phrase, that dehumanizes Black women and masks the systemic harms that disproportionately put Black women in positions that necessitate ridiculous amounts of "strength." I take that critique in no way lightly, as the Strong Black Woman is a caricatured image that deeply impacts how we see and interact with—or don't—Black women. But while I take that critique, I maintain, too, its misguidedness here. This piece is not

III.

Who does, or more specifically *can*, speak for whom? A contentious question, especially in the realms of the historically marginalized. When epidermally white people have spoken for folks of Color ("The Negroes are a [insert monolithic characteristic here] people"), or when (cis) men have spoken for women ("See, the thing about women is . . ." the frat dudebro pontificates), or when cis folks have spoken for trans folks ("The transsexual experiences a state of gender dysphoria that causes . . ."), the result has been overwhelmingly detrimental to the marginalized. Hegemonic subjectivities have had dangerous effects.

Such language deployed in the vicinity of the marginalized works to harm them while supporting the integrity of the dominant group.

---

about Black women; it is about *Black feminism*, a distinction I want to contentiously highlight: Black women are not the all of, or a synonym for, Black feminism. It is intentional and crucial to note that what this piece discusses primarily is the *legacy* that the Black woman whom I note at the outset cites, as it were; it is a legacy that can be inhabited by those who choose to take up the characteristics of that legacy. I highlight *the work* of Black radical feminism, emphasizing that it is the performative and agential politics to which one commits oneself that is my interest, a politics that, by virtue of (porous) structural positionings, has historically been done out of necessity by those who identify or are identified as Black women. And further still, I note unequivocally my "insistence on Black feminism," which is a disposition, a way of inhabiting the world disruptively, rather than a static identity that one is born with—that is, "being" a Black woman. I am less interested in reifying things Black women have said and touting those, by mere fact of their articulation by someone Black and woman, as Black feminist utterances, and much, much more interested in how excavating a fugitive force of refusal that supervenes on historically contingent valences—that is, irruptions that have been consolidated, porously, onto those who are deemed to be Black and/or woman—opens up this tortuous space for thinking fugitive political subjectivity (subjectivity as such) and possibility differently, on the fissuring edge of normative narratives. So, no, I am not further perpetuating the myth of the Strong Black Woman. I am talking about that Black feminist life.

For a cis person to misgender someone bears much less on the livelihood and subjectivity of the cis person than on those of the, say, trans
person who has been misgendered. The misgendering could result in
trans fatality, but rarely—or, in reality, never—will such a misgendering result in much harm to the cis person. There is an ethics, then, to
how the language of Blackness, queerness, and (nonnormative) gender identities is deployed in general, and more specifically by those
who are not Black, trans, or gender-nonconforming. Put differently,
language *does* things, and it is lived differently, experienced differently, by different people, necessitating care when deploying it. People
are affected, people come into existence, and people are erased when
certain language is used. And furthermore, language dictates what we
can and do know. Language is the very conduit for our *subjectivation*
as well as the breadth of our knowledge.

Hence, when writing, reading, speaking, and thinking about Blackness or transness in particular, about queerness or Black feminism in
general, it is imperative that these axioms be noted and be constitutive
of what we then do with how we think and write and speak about
Blackness and transness. Especially those who, like me, are placed in
hegemonic positions by way of how others perceive their identities.
Such a task is both necessary and deeply fraught for me, for a number of reasons. But because of the ethics of the struggle to which we
commit ourselves, tarrying in the space between deference and intellectual confidence/steadfastness, and between wanting to recalibrate
cherished identities and thinking about the ethics of whether that is
something I am even permitted to do, is troubled terrain. Good, I say,
let it be troubled, and *troubling*, because that is, in fact, where I must
remain—and where my thinking urges me and others to dwell.

In short, the conventional wisdom deserves respect but also, I timidly
claim, critique. The spirit of critique, that Marxian ruthless criticism of
all that exists, rests at the fundament of the politics to which I adhere—a
politics most precisely captured by the elegantly wild commingling of

the Blackness and transness and feminism of it all. I want to offer a deferential departure from the conventional wisdom, and this departure might rub a few folks wrongly. The nature of my departure, though, is one shrouded in love, and this loving departure, its fundamental critical disposition, demands space to speak. So, here goes.

I begin and end many of my thoughts with Cathy Cohen, because her intellect has for years had my love. Her recalibration of queerness in her landmark essay "Punks, Bulldaggers, and Welfare Queens" urges rethought modes of inhabitation. Cohen helpfully broadens our understanding of queerness by arguing that queerness, instead of being an identity that sexually and gender-divergent folks possess, should be understood as an orientation, as a relation to power. In short, queerness, for Cohen, concerns "political identities"— identities formed around what we do, how we disrupt, and, in more fuzzy emotional terms (though no less rigorous ones), where our hearts are; identities "rooted not in our shared history or identity but in our shared marginal relationship to dominant power that normalizes, legitimizes, and privileges."[8] That is, it's all well and good (a phrasing my mother loves to use) to think about the specificity of social, material, and psychic phenomena that betide those who are read and interpreted as Black or trans or women (or all three), as this has historical import (e.g., with respect to the possibility of reparations bestowed, representation, affirmative action, anti-Black/trans violence stemming from legal and extralegal State apparatuses, etc.), but this ain't enough for me because these identities do not end at the violence done to them nor are they captured entirely by such violence. It thus necessitates, perhaps, thinking of the Black, the trans, the queer, *additionally* (not solely, though perhaps more substantively), as "the destabilization and remaking of our identities" and a mode of putting in work with others not simply by way of skin color, gender expression, or sex designation, but by a proclivity to "challenge and bring together all those deemed marginal and all those committed to liberatory politics," *only a facet of which* manifests on the body as legible markers of common identities.

I want to foreground iconoclastic fluidity and fugitive movement not beholden to racial and gender optics; I want to foreground the interrogation of deeply regulated and putatively unchangeable identities, and the willingness to relinquish legibility—how we (think we) look—in favor of political nega-legibility—how we do ourselves in subversion of hegemony. My concern, my interest, my argument is less in whose purported blood runs through the veins of your ancestral genealogy, or what genitalia / secondary sex characteristics / hormones / chromosomes / name-your-proxy-for-gender-identity you have, and more on where your politics are. As Kai M. Green so forcefully and succinctly writes: *What do your politics look like? And what kind of work do you do?*[9]

Of course I'm not arguing that trans studies is something that only trans people can participate in. Far from it—anybody can develop an expertise in this area, or feel that they have some sort of stake in it.

— Susan Stryker, "Transgender Studies Today:
An Interview with Susan Stryker"

At what point are we deemed appropriately qualified to work within the knowledge aligned with a particular demographic? The claim that I or other folks who are read as cis cannot speak about trans subjectivity, or that I cannot and should not be doing trans studies, largely comes from a place of hesitance about cis people occupying trans spaces—physical or epistemological. It is a necessary claim to circulate, especially since trans folks have developed very keen ways of detecting threats to their livelihood. What happens, though, when we take seriously the knowledge taking hold in trans studies that *trans* denotes less a specific gendered body and more a movement away from an originary, imposed starting point? Transness manifests, in the first instance, as an elusive capacity that cannot be discerned by making recourse to the visual or normative. Reified definitions of trans and cis, even Black and white, and so on, cannot hold indefinitely and have no clearly discernible threshold of distinction. Transness, as not solely or in the first instance about the material gendered body, might mark a way of relating to which transgender people have an "(under)privileged" access.

I am working on and struggling with mobilizing this rigorous kind of trans politics as a way to inhabit and encounter the world. This is Kai M. Green again influencing me: trans is "a decolonial demand," a move to decolonize gender; "a question of how, when, and where one sees and knows; a reading practice that might help readers gain a reorientation to orientation."[10] This is a struggle to note that when cis folks show up to trans spaces we need to do just that—*show up*, in the vernacular sense of bringing your A game, knowing your shit, puttin' in work. You get nothing just for being at the party; no cookies, no applause, no praise for being able to say, "I was at a drag ball last weekend." If you claim solidarity and coalition with the radical effects of trans, you better know how the *DSM* functions to pathologize trans subjectivity as a disorder and what that might mean for trans folks who seek gender confirmation surgery; you better know that survival sex work affects how some trans people (primarily trans women of Color) relate to sex; you better know that trans folks often risk their lives simply by going outside after dark (or during the day); you better know that you gon' constantly have to practice getting pronouns right, and that those pronouns might change tomorrow; you better know that your very cis presence may exude hostility in trans spaces (hell, in all spaces) and it's valid for trans folks to be super-suspicious; you better know that trans communities are not just surgeries and surveillance and imminent violence but joy and boisterousness and *life being lived*; you better know that there is so much more that you cannot know; and you better know, too, that you don't know shit.

Yet my thoughts don't end here. And this is where it gets thorny, where the radicality of radical politics begins to lose some friends. We must remember that cisness is not simply a possessed identity or fixed location on the body; it is determined as well by relative effect. So when I write about trans subjectivity as a cis(-ish) man I may, maybe, perhaps, be undoing that "cisness" by virtue of thinking *with* trans because the effects of my cisness are unsuturing the seams of that cisness and cisnormativity. My cisness, especially in my writing, does not stay in the proper place of cisness—it has and must continue to have a disruptive effect that undoes cisness itself. Cisness, and transness, can "speak out of character," a necessity for dismantling the reified statuses these identities exude, which are the result of cisnormativity fixing identities into unchanging hierarchical castes. And further, because many trans folks do not undergo surgical intervention, which would mark a clearer (though still flawed) distinction between trans and cis, it is still unsettled where cis ends and trans begins. Blurring an already blurred line makes for some gender trouble. And this, to me, is always to say that gender loses its coherency when Blackness shows up to the party, which is to say it has always already showed up to the party, acting a fool and getting buck. (Addendum: The production of cisgender, too, disallows nuanced conversation about the complexity within it. A question or two: If Blackness is always already queer, am I a "proper" cis subject? If Black [cis] women have long been disallowed the category of "woman," is a [cis] Black woman wholly and fittingly within that category?)

Sometimes I want to ask with my eyes cast down, a timid whimper in my voice: "What if a Cohen-inspired queer posture, a norm-contesting politics," as Lyndon K. Gill ventures, "provides the definitive criteria by which a life, a work, a process counts as queer?"; "Does aligning ourselves with the philosophical spirit and rebellious fortitude of progressive deviants make us queer regardless of non-normative desire or sex/gender 'transgressions'?"[11] Can the same, or something similar, be said of trans if it, too, is a queer posture? If it is true that no one can fully inhabit a gender (especially "without a degree of horror," per Denise Riley[12]), nor can anyone be soaked in awareness of their gender 24/7, is it possible to, in those moments of non-soakedness, in those flickers of my desaturated cisness—itself an unstable term, to be sure—find (under)common ground with trans folks? Is the *work* of trans studies a means by which I do necessary violence to my cisness, resulting in moments of coalitional viability, moments of, effectively, being-with transness? If trans is a mode of seeing and saying and disorienting, might it someday be possible to not *be* but to be-with trans, even despite my purported cisness?

I shudder in quiet boldness imagining the possibilities.

I emailed Marlon B. Ross back in January of 2015. I loved his book *Manning the Race* and wanted to simply express my gratitude to him. And he was kind. I asked him how one grapples with one's privileged, hegemonic identities when doing work about/with people and places to which one has no experiential claim. The more categories of identity that we are called on to negotiate, he said, the more we can feel immobilized while trying to do and say the right thing in a world that often feels deeply unchanged around numerous issues. But the task, he said, is to never see one's embodiment or subjectivity as a burden. The task is to deploy one's subjectivity in subversive ways. What I understood from the rest of his lengthy message is that it matters less that one say the "right" thing and more that one be a "wrong" proper subject. How can I think and be and disrupt *with* trans even in the moments when I am read as cis? These are the possibilities, the radical, open possibilities, that Blackness as disobedience, or queerness as opposition to power, or transness as fugitive transmogrifying posture, or feminism as critical, subversive reading of inscriptions of race and gender bring about. And possibility—as illegible and fraught and terrifying as it is—is what I am after.

So, believe it or not, I am called to be guided by ethics. Our work is ethical in its hegemonic unethicality; our work, if it thinks with those marginalized and erased folks, is indecorous in the face of power, and in this sense I maintain an ethical posture with respect to those who are marginalized. I cannot hide behind decorum, for this only maintains dominative systems of varying degrees of normativity. I need to conspire against such systems, which is to say be an accomplice to the outlaw whose being has been cast as impossible and unwanted. If the Law is unjust, the only just mode of being is outlawry—outside the Law. We may have different histories and different lived experiences, but we can conspire to raise hell together.

I like to think I get it: there are some who are chained, and those chains hurt. As well, there are some with chained wrists, but others with chained wrists and ankles, and still others with chained wrists, ankles, and necks. Our chains demand sympathy, demand outrage, demand the recognition "I see your chains." I think it is my aim, though, to see those chains but understand that chainedness is not where it ends. Because, of course, many let their chains sit comfortably about them, even reshackling them when they slip off. We feel formed and shaped by the nature of our chains, their texture and grit intimate friends of ours. The ways we are categorized, and categorize ourselves, give us a shape in the world, the removal of which would thrust us into catastrophic shapelessness. But be not alarmed when I say that we have all been betrayed by the masqueraded good-naturedness of our chains, our categorizations—one and the very same. Perhaps what I demand as I menacingly clutch the promises of fugitivity is *forever, a new act of creation, which can save us*.[13] This critical recalibration, the Blackness of Blackness, its abiding fugitive feminism, its indispensable queerness—the liberatory miasma of its flesh—is the opening act of a new creation. My aim is dwelling with the lives and thoughts of those whose chains are perpetually rattling. And to those without chains or with fewer chains, my aim is to see if they, say, tell those chain-deniers about the pervasive presence of chains, or if they make keys for chains, or if they choose to commune with those dreaded chained people. *That* is what I stake my claim in.

A Series of (Un)related Events*

Black feminism is a double refusal: the refusal to disappear and the refusal to comply.

— Denise Ferreira da Silva, "Hacking the Subject: Black Feminism, Refusal, and the Limits of Critique"

I t starts without context. They are cast as insane, volatile, undeserving of sympathy for their unjust outrage stemming from who-knows-what. No one can know because it stems from nowhere, this rage, or rather anger, a hissy fit. Because rage is built up, resting on a solid foundation of reason. "You've gone mad, mad, I tell you, mad." *Ni-Ni-Nicki she just mad . . . .* "Oh my god, she's gone crazy," they say, because crazy isn't crazy for a reason. It's just crazy. Dungeoned dragons, they are. *Raah, raah.*

This has been the narrative constructing the dominant image of Black women, monolithically consolidated into Hottentot caricatures. Experiences comprised of a series of (un)related events: outrage that is the product of a historical legacy of erasure and straight-up disses—individual, institutional, imagistic, you name it—is construed as coming "out of nowhere"; social and economic penury that is the result of gendered labor opportunities and racially motivated geographic and career foreclosures is erased from cultural memory. Black women

---

*An earlier version of this essay originally appeared on *The Feminist Wire* on February 3, 2016.

cannot become, or more accurately cannot reinvent themselves as, acceptable subjects, because to be seen, to be recognized, as human, as valid bodily matter, is to be accepted as a citizen. And to be a citizen, in the United States at least, is, as Claudia Rankine says, to "come on. Let it go. Move on."[1]

"Let it go. Let it gooo!" Elsa sings in *Frozen*, a Disney flick that had everybody—like, *everybody*—geekin' for months on end. We are urged to let everything go, get away from the past, from what has gotten us here. Become "one with the wind and sky," don't think about this earth, this ground that is saturated with the blood and sweat of those whose names we shall not speak. Only "the storm" is allowed to "rage on." Indifferent and indiscriminate weather catastrophes are permitted to rage, not people who have been wronged by other people and assert their personhood in the face of its plunder. "The past is in the past," Elsa sings, and that is where all those who have benefited from the past's horrors would like to keep it. Related to everything, but not. (Un)related.

A woman I used to date, a Black woman whose tenacity is unmatched, whose intellect exudes a genuineness that makes stability quake, feared my rejection of her hair. Until then, she had only let me see her with extensions, with a weave. Still her hair, nevertheless, it needs to be stated, 'cause y'all say buying anything else makes it yours to own, but let a Black woman buy her hair and suddenly "it's not really hers." Trepidation clutched her and history mocked her. And they almost won.

"Babe, please don't be upset with yourself," I pleaded in a text. The vibration—one, two, three, a four-page SMS haunted by a teetering textual lachrymosity—was hefty with a desire, a plea, to be seen, and to be loved nonetheless. "You've inherited (well, we've all inherited) a legacy of a cultural environment that denigrates Black women's hair. Your reasoning is in no way stupid—it is a keen understanding of the historical. But I promise you that I will neither think less of you, nor love you less, nor ask you to ever change anything about your appearance for me. While I have my issues with the prioritizing of standardized aesthetic beauty as that which implicitly validates people, I'll say this, and I mean it: you are beautiful to me, whether bald or with the locks of Samson. You may be nervous, which is fine, but I guarantee that I will still look at you in utter awe and love you the way I have been."

I can only hope that she believed me. Though the narrative of history, justifiably, may tell her to be skeptical.

To claim the denigrated, to love the purportedly unlovable, to dare to believe that Blackness is enough is a toast to living, to surviving, to stealing life from a world that continuously tells you not to be. Her hair, then, is a ruthlessly garnered site of parrhesia. Bold speech. I am here. I will be. And I will be all of me. "The natural is sacrilegious," Cenen Moreno says in "Ebony Minds, Black Voices." And white/male supremacy is the religious law of the blood-saturated land.

Toni Cade Bambara's *The Black Woman: An Anthology* was published in 1970. Coincidentally, or perhaps not, that was the year my mother was born. I wonder if she's read it. I doubt it. But that only means she hasn't seen the words combined in script on off-white pages whispering back to her. Mom knows everything in the book, I imagine. Eleanor Traylor, in her introduction to the 2005 edition, says *The Black Woman* is comprised of "inscribed conversations that emerge from the kitchen." And Mom was in the kitchen, with Grandma, conversing, speaking, inventing. One of the joys of my childhood as a young Black boy surrounded by grown-ass Black women was listening to this invention. As I eavesdropped, I witnessed history, quite literally, being made. I kept my eyes on their world, paid attention to what went on.

And here I am, a conduit for their truths, writing it all down, every detail, inscribing voices that have sent me here to do their will.

They lived hard. Living is a process of rebellion. It is a fugitive praxis of daring to exist, a double refusal that the site of Black and woman engages by neither leaving nor complying. Living in the face of imposed death, sanctioned death, beatified death, is itself liberatory. And it is a struggle on all fronts. Black women turning to one another, revolutionarily and familially, is rebellion. Insurgence. Chaos. And transformative revolution lays its head in chaos. That turning toward one another invents bonds.

My mother only occasionally showed effusive loving affection. But she lived in love, always. I used to forget that this life is not merely about pain, injustice, being dissed. Love exists too. Marlon B. Ross responded to an email I once sent him when I became steeped in Black pain: *I think we sometimes overlook in our theory how identification brings pleasure and how pleasure itself can disrupt unjust hierarchies of identity*, he said. *Taking pleasure in being a black straight male or a black queer male or whatever does not mean contentment with hierarchies that cause oppression; it means using the pleasure that comes from social differentiation (of all kinds) against those hierarchies.*

And in gifting me with those words, Marlon loved me. If only I had listened, seen, felt what my mother was expressing all along, I could have spent more time seeing more love.

October 26, 2015. Spring Valley High School, Columbia, South Carolina: I wonder if, when he woke up and put on his uniform—protecting and serving—he said to himself he'd carry the torch of white male brutality against Black women's bodies. Which is to say the torch of white masculinity. Which is to say the torch of whiteness. Which is to say the torch of America with a capital "'Merica."

I wonder if she, Shakara, exhausted as on any other day, thought that she'd have to justify, once again, her existence, her self-possession. Which is to say I wonder if she thought to herself, *I exist in this world as a Black woman. Round 6,570.*

Deputy Fields—powerlifter like me, white unlike me, subject to the smog of male supremacy like me, bred in the cauldron of America like us all—was performing a routine. "Either you come with me or I'll make you," he said. And Blackness, of course, never submits willingly. The "I'll make you" referenced, too, the shoehorning of this Black woman into "The Black Woman," the "hoodrat," the "nigger bitch," the chattel. Movable property. *Partus sequitur ventrem* in the flesh.

No need to give her time to get up, to move herself—she wasn't going to. Or she didn't have to. Or she wasn't supposed to. Take her down, the desk too. Slam her again for good (or bad) measure. Drag her, put her on display for all to see—or not. Was she seen? A classmate, Niya Kenny—another Black woman, the only one to say something in response to the violence occurring—yelled, "What the fuck?! What the fuck?! This can't happen." Was she seen? Who was seen? What was seen?

Don't dare interrupt whiteness, maleness at work. "I'll put you in jail next," Fields said to someone, maybe Niya, maybe not. He wasn't talking only about himself. He wasn't talking only about the other student either.

The papers say the woman wasn't hurt. But they don't know that. They don't know what else happened decades, centuries ago. Just then or yesterday. To her or not. It all blends together as if it's all the same thing, at the same time, to the same person. Sometimes it is. Most times it is too.

I saw the video, as with most other twentysomethings' doses of national news, on Facebook. "No! You are not serious right now, yo," I said to myself, chillin' in my bed, clad in my hoodie, wanting to unsee. Or to see again, but differently. I emailed the sheriff, re: The Unacceptable Behavior of Deputy Ben Fields:

> As I hope your department knows, Deputy Ben Fields was recorded using unnecessary, violent, incessant force fomented, I would assert, by his adherence to discourses that cast Black bodies as threatening, criminal, and unruly. Deputy Fields, mired, no doubt, in the arrogance and legacy of his white masculinity—exacerbated by the state-sanctioned authority of a badge—enacted that white masculinity onto a Black female body, denigrating its integrity, validity, and right to exist *boldly* in public educational space. That Deputy Fields acted in such a violent and abusive manner toward this Black woman—who was in no way physically threatening—should not be condoned. Know that this is no isolated incident; that this is buttressed by a precedent of white men violating Black female bodies for their own glorification and racial and gendered valorization.
>
> I request that, because of his unconscionable actions, he be removed from the force (an ironic term, no?).
>
> Please act on this, as the reputation of your department, as well as law enforcement writ large, is at stake.
>
> This is not protecting and serving; this is violating and abusing.

No "Best," no "Sincerely," no "Regards," warmest or otherwise.

And he was removed from the department.

But as I reread it I feel like I went too easy on him. Why did I say "please"? Why did I "request"? Why am I asking? Was I charmed by whiteness again? Well, let me revise and demand instead. I provide no option, and the consequences, I assure you, are dire.

Which is to say, as Joshua Bennett does, "When I say, 'I do not believe in Hell, but there are nonetheless men, dead and living, I wish Hell upon,' understand I am first a historian of suffering."[2] We—she much more than me, much more than so-called "us"—have suffered. At the hands of many incarnations of Deputy Fields. So if I may pretend I am a believer, even though I am not, even though right now that is all I am: I, unapologetically, wish Hell upon you.

If you stand still too long, they will put chains on you, so you want to keep moving. . . . The true freedom in the slave narrative is at the point of deciding to escape and the journey north . . . the freedom that people experience is actually when they are on the road, in flight.

— Harryette Mullen, "Interview with Harryette Mullen"

As embedded in, and a manifestation of, Black feminism, Harryette Mullen's poetry is fugitive. She knows very well that "they will put chains on you," and her work in all its forms is to flee those chains. Her poetic corpus is an invitation to what one scholar calls her "fugitive run," but the aim of this running is to be located not in an achieved state of freedom but in the particular moment of "the point of [the slave's] *deciding to escape*," as she says in the epigraph above. Freedom and fugitivity remain "elusive, momentary, and a state of mind; it is discursive rather than related to the location of the body."[3] Freedom, in other words, occurs at the moment of escape, at the moment of fugitivity. It becomes an on-the-run-ness, indexed by those fugitive slaves who eluded capture in myriad ways. To inhabit Blackness becomes to inhabit elusiveness.

This is, too, a Black feminist dwelling space, a tactic to evade capture. In the context of pervasive surveillance, which takes the form of literal biometric regulatory regimes as well as metaphysical, ontological, epistemological, historical, documentary, interpersonal, and social mechanisms, Blackness and its gender trouble—a Black feminist apparatus of knowing—is always excessive. When surveillance happens, though, there is always something outside its scope, something beyond the edges of its frame. Black feminism insists that frames can't hold or contain, because Black feminism's historical (though not sole) archetype, Black women, exceeds the axioms of representation and exceeds full capture within a frame. Black women—or rather, fugitive Black feminism—cannot be fixed in representation; Black feminist fugitivity refuses being cordoned, being framed, because it defies elaboration. Fundamentally transformative, Black feminist fugitivity enacts a perpetual off-tilted, off-kilter being-and-becoming-in-the-world. The movement of Blackness references Sarah Jane Cervenak's "black movement" because it is "*read* as disruptive physicality."[4] Blackness's disruption of physicality indexes what Cervenak calls wandering, a response to the stultifying logics of the kinds of movements that are permitted to be visible in public and a pervasive "antiwandering ethos targeted particularly at the nonnormative"—the Black, the queer, the trans, the fugitive. To wander is "the errancy of queerness and the queerness of errancy"; it is "unruly bodies. Unruly desires."

I want to put my faith in the forces compelling these Black women, forces that have created a Black feminism of radical disorientation, of rupture that will call forth new worlds and new peoples that we do not yet have names for and may never have language for, because they may never be able to be hailed into this world. Black feminism moves in and through the interstices (the gotten-in-between), and, in that in-between, movement disrupts fixity. Vibrantly disruptive, it is livelihood, life that exists between—always between and unincorporated into—regimes. A kind of *interregnal* Black feminism. This is not merely a vibrancy and complexity amid positional abjection, nor is it simply life within (social) death; it is, I prefer, life through and through, irrespective of (indeed, unconcerned with) definitional scripts that apportion life and death. To exist in a lively way in the interregnum is to proclaim that the interregnum is the place where life happens and from where generative forces build. Black feminism might be the doing of life in the interregnum, in the suspension of governing rules and logics—literally between reigns.

And this has been evident in our midst already: from the enslaved's womb being a "factory reproducing blackness as abjection and turning the birth canal into another domestic middle passage," while all the while it was still, in that Black feminist double refusal, "difficult, if not impossible, to assimilate black women's domestic labors and reproductive capacities";[5] to gender-nonconforming folks rolling up 150 strong to Dewey's Famous coffee shop in Philadelphia, Pennsylvania—a hangout for Black queer and trans folks in the city from which I hail—and demanding that the establishment cease its policy of refusing service to those in "non-conformist clothing" (a linguistic proxy for fugitive genders); to the kitchen table, the stove with boiling pots of good cookin', the gay laughter; to the insurgence of Black women's writing in the 1970s, showcasing, archetypally, how, though all the women were white and all the Blacks men, some of them were Black-woman-brave and possessed "tongues of fire," incendiary knowledge, hostile epistemologies even, that were "your linguistic nightmare, your linguistic aberration";[6] to Tourmaline's insistence on "foreground[ing] this *knowledge* . . . that an investment in biologically determined gender is an investment in identities that were violently imposed on our bodies in order to maintain capitalism, white supremacy and colonialism";[7] to the seemingly mundane sharing of a blog post, video, essay, article, or status by our Black/woman/trans/queer kinfolk on Facebook or Twitter. These knowledges that act in defiance are deemed invalid, and deemed valid only when they can fit the dominant narrative, which is to say, largely, when they are digested by the hegemonic bowels of verification and thoroughly assimilated. It is Black radical women—all of whom are possibly different inflections of the same anoriginally lawless phenomenon—who have long theo-rized the place that demands a demand, a place that is, in fact, a debt: *our queer debt, our black debt, our trans debt*.[8] And these are debts that we cannot possibly, because they are impossible, repay. Preserve the impossibility, the unassimilability, as that will ensure an inventiveness and truly open up those spaces feared by State powers. Those spaces are our salvation.

An ode to the way Black women make resilience a craft. To the way Black women hurt, cry, feel weak, grow exhausted, don't want to take care of anyone. An ode to their vulnerability, their imperfection, their flaws. They are strong, yes. And they are unceasingly weak. And everywhere in between.

An ode to how Black women sing when no one is listening, because that is when they can listen to themselves live within the all of them-selves. When those Black girls, like my sister, snaggle-toothed and full of life, jump rope and chant among themselves, they are build-ing monuments to genealogical artisans who looked just like them, who spoke like them, who let out sighs of exasperation heavy with the weight of being in their bodies. Can you hear them, singing, humming—the *pneuma* of Black womanhood flourishing?

An ode to those Black women whose names have been left off the record of history, whose efforts went unseen. You were integral, I promise. And I give thanks. An ode, because imagining oneself, inventing oneself, is a rebellious act.

Scenes of Illegible Shadow Genders

They* traverse the Commons like an enigma, an insurgent mystery, a mobile question mark disrupting the typical goings-on of the college town. Headphones on, eyes closed sometimes, rarely acknowledging the presence of other bodies or stares or cell-phone recordings of their gyrations, their fugitive movements. They are sometimes without a shirt, their skin on unapologetic display; often in compression shorts and Ugg boots; often swaying

---

*I use and will likely always use, barring a self-determined revelation on their part, the gender-nonbinary pronoun *they* to speak of this person. To do otherwise would be a violence to the very thing, it seems to me, they are attempting to do: exude in their performative motions a gendered illegibility. The nonbinary *they* facilitates this wish and aims at a kind of nondescription, or an open description vulnerable to the unknown, the unanticipated, and the uncapturable. *They* refuses the urge to afflict this person with a gendered ontology, this dweller in the (under)Commons; indeed, in the undercommons, in which this person, I think, has a mobile home and *mobile* home, the language of gender as we know it cannot hold. *They* is thus my closest approximation to an unholdable and unheld gender. *They* is a scene of an illegible shadow gender.

eloquently, carelessly; sometimes lying on the ground, swiveling their hips, singing, singing, singing. And sometimes they have sunglasses on, and in those moments I can't see their eyes, which are sometimes accented with blood-red, tear-shaped stains. I wonder what the world looks like to them. I wonder what they look like to themselves. My urge to ask their name, or to invent one for my own personal cognitive records, belies their unnameability. Once a friend of mine tried to ask this person's name, but they refused, only shook their head and continued listening to something somewhere else. A shadow realm whispering robust ciphers. I cannot name them, though I try. I wish to know them, yet that is precisely what I cannot do. Let them remain enigmatic as they grind on the obelisk in their compression shorts and Uggs, quite literally moving to the beat of their own tune. Let the question of their being remain unanswered as they amble about public space, mouthing song lyrics to themselves, perhaps literally in their own world. I would assert that they are not in this space: they are in the undercommons, reveling in the cacophony, the tumultuous sludge of vivacious unrecognizability, the boisterous underside of "Culture."

They are a dweller in the undercommons—or, more precisely, a dweller in the (under)Commons—inhabiting the public space of, tellingly, my college town's "Commons." I wonder what it is this person wants. What do fugitive dwellers in the (under)Commons want—or, one might ask, *how* do they want, what *don't* they want, what, to the fugitive, does "want" even mean?

In one sense, then, they are an outlaw, a deviant from the perspective of the common Law, a breaker of hegemonic rules, one who has busted out of the joint. They are outlaw—outside the Law—ungoverned, unruly, baaadddasss.

Rejecting the State-sanctioned norms of public space—a space that is governed by gender norms and rules about how bodies can and should appear—the dweller in the (under)Commons in my college town, as a veritable fugitive, perhaps even, I would argue, *queer*, seizes public space, a space, by virtue of its publicness, that is normatively marked. They are sinful. They seize the space, queer it, and lay claim to the right to *appear*—or not, strategically or desultorily dissembling and deploying their unintelligibility—thus challenging both racial and gendered assumptions of space.

Yooo, that nigga gay or somethin'? I heard one person say. *He [sic] got them feminine nut-huggers on and shit, my nigga,* the person's friend responded. Their comments are telling. The dweller in the (under)Commons, entirely unfazed by these, or any, onlookers, was being hailed by these two. The two men—deeply invested in their manness, feeding it to one another—distinctly racialized and masculinized the dweller, and in so doing tried to relegate the dweller to a pathological identity of abjection, a racial and gender identity implied to be incompatible with their understanding of the dweller's body. But, vetoing that noise because they were living in noise, the dweller in the (under)Commons utterly refused the validity of the normative logic. They continued to grind away, to listen to the music that no one else could hear. By appearing in public space precisely as a troubling body that is assumed to be disallowed from the realm of the public, they laid claim to the public while simultaneously occupying their undercommons.

The dweller in the (under)Commons refuses to comply with the Law—the Law of categorizable bodies, the Law of public propriety, the Law of proper gendered performances. The dweller in the (under)Commons holds, in their subjectivity, heat that conflagrates normative space. They embody volatility. Put boldly and simply, the dweller in the (under)Commons is a fuckin' problem. A gendered outlaw, they exist para-lawlessly and question the logic of laws presumed to be infallible, fixed, axiomatic. What, then, does this do to how we all inhabit the world? What possibilities might this present for us? Might the dweller in the (under)Commons be making an attempt to liberate us?

This dweller provides an occasion, here, to imagine the other stuff that might be somewhere else. The dweller is a scene, a twinkle from another here that we might look toward for otherwise-gendered subjectivities, gendered subjectivities ruled by unruly goon rules. Goon genders, if you will (and even if you will not). These are the genders to which the radical feminist calls, and if the call is heartfelt and genuine enough, courageous enough, there may be the faintest of responses, faint by necessity because its voice breaks our aural grammars, only permitted to fleetingly echo. If they were to respond just a tad louder, what might they, possibly, say of themselves?

Ecstasis, *a word in the etymological chain of* ecstasy, *was used in 1656 by John Smith. In his* Compleat Practice of Physick, *Smith wrote: "Ecstasis is either true, as when the mind is drawn away to contemplate heavenly things, or [etc.]." To be beside oneself—ecstatic—is a generative state. Upon first reading Smith's sentence, we stared at the nodes on either side of the subclause. And to be honest, we are less interested in the veracity of ecstasis, whatever Smith took that to mean (something divine, we suppose). Truthfully, we were, and are still, drawn to the "or [etc.]." We are drawn to its function as the untrue, distinct from false and, to our mind, a signifier of a different kind of proximity to what is. And we are drawn to the etc., how it has to be bracketed out, corralled and contained, quarantined from the seamlessness of the sentence's grammar. Might the etc., not even able to occupy unqualified space in the sentence, needing to be sequestered away somewhere else, be a way to get outside of getting outside of?*

We are constantly trying to get outside of ourselves, which is already an attempt to get outside of. Because that's where it starts. In trickles or dashes with a stammering babble, the intimacy with which we do this is corrosive. Strangely, we know you are not yet ours, and have never been. Not yet. But there is still a thoroughgoing intimacy. We were born

together, but you've been born time and again. Even as we share an
intimacy begotten by a virulent estrangement we are not called mad.
But we are, or want to be.

I am thinking of a moment. Or rather, a scale. The Kelvin scale, a thermodynamic temperature scale invented by William Thomson (also known as Lord Kelvin), is among the three standards for measuring temperature. It is at base an instrument of capture, though an admittedly rather benign one. It measures, describes, nothing more. It is an instrument wholly given to what it attends to, attending without need for return. And yet it still presumes.

The Kelvin scale has only one fixed point—absolute zero, which is 273 degrees Celsius colder than the freezing temperature of water. But the term is a misnomer; absolute zero is not absolute. Absolute zero is the lowest measurable temperature, at which molecules trudge as slowly as they might possibly move. But even there, in the absoluteness of null, the absolute is not absolute. Molecules still move. *There are zeroes beneath zeroes.*[1] There is a world of movement occurring imperceptibly. The instruments we have for observation, even when they market themselves as passive measures of neutrality, presumptuously set limits to what they presume are the boundaries of legibility. Beneath Kelvin's absolute zero that is far from absolute is a world in the shadows, moving beneath the barometric radar. That movement is unreadable and untrackable. That movement is where we might want to move.

It's a strange desire that we often have, a desire that seeks absolutes and bedrocks. Little is gained when we delimit those absolutes, and more is stalled. Such rigidity in the absolute. So little room. Thankfully, absoluteness refuses its own absoluteness. Zero is more than zero. Zero has another name, and another. So there is something beneath it all, and beneath "all" there is something that persists despite the overbearing kibosh. Can it speak? Can we hear its whispers? What is its language; what are the contours of its illegibility? More aptly, we must wonder what motion and stillness, singing and dancing, feeling and hearing are like in the nonzero of the absolute. We need a new metric for gauging (how things happen) differently. The scales we have, Kelvins and otherwise, cannot get at that other thing, that thing below the bottom. It will take an unscaled scale. And this scale is the conduit that shuttles us through a byzantine darkness where we need to learn to see through the night of the general benightedness. There we'll find, if we dare to look where we couldn't look, if we dare to feel around in the forbidden, habitable glimmers that shine darkly.

Your attempts, failingly, to describe us, to describe where we roam, are little more than teeny marionettes rehearsing their monologues for absent audiences, unaware that their strings are being torqued (or that they have strings), unmoving, soulless eyes staring. We confess this to you because it is all we can do, the closest approximation to a warning.

That's how we stole ourselves, that's how we got out. Held captive by what we thought birthed us, because it did, which was the onset of our sentence, its syntactic strictures, its grammatical grip. Forbidden from going elsewhere. We had to get out, if only to get in it again. But it's hard to get out, to even know there's an out to be gotten to. We think here loves us. We think here is lush. Here exerts a torsion on us that neither immobilizes nor strangles. And we are grateful, thankful that we are cage-free in an openness, free-range on a range of arrangements. All of it, though, at base, is an originary theft.

So we steal ourselves back, beyond. With underground detraining and subterranean undiscipline, we steal ourselves, on the sly, secretively so as not to secrete the secret of the selves they didn't know we had and didn't know we knew of. Repeat it at your own risk; repetition requires a mappable matrix the grid of which is their radar. Don't repeat it.

Don't repeat it. There it is again, trying to steal our stealing. Trying to claim as contraband that which was contraband. We only abscond again with stolen goods to territories unknown and dangerous—(you've been warned)—because the serpents and dragons of terra incognita are our threshold.

Flickering scenes that allusively glimpse the illegibility of gender's shadow realm. Therein, maybe, lies the rubbed-out possibility that *is* the rubbed-out. When looking for presence we, a priori, shun the possibility of the very thing, the non-thing, that coaxed us, whisperingly, in the first place. Claim the dispossession and we might finally possess-without-possessing what we long for. Claim ourselves as dispossessed and we might finally become what we might have become. Then let go of the urge to claim.

What we try to sing, scratching away paint chips in search of that underground, is a porous and dewy guttural residue. Because *shadows linger and leak. They seep from mottled grey and scaffold scalar recollections. They assure our potential, securing it by ways and means at once penumbral and exquisite. They instantiate things remembered past their time, promised beyond situation.*[2] The shadows of what we might become, their anoriginary filmic negative. In the shadows.

These shadows linger and leak by staying with us and spilling from the cracks in what we have been given. Even when gone, the shadows were there; they remain even after they leave (*ghosted shadows*) and make messes. Don't clean up the mess, please. I've always been notoriously apathetic when it comes to minor spills and trifling messes. It's only because I desire a way to live cleanly in that mess.

Where is the place with those different ways to inhabit? Hiding in the shadows, I'd bet, or lurking in the dark corners—or rather, the dark spaces, because this place has no use for corners, only space. Open space, unbounded space that can't be touched quite yet, not under these conditions. It's a spacey space, a space unspaced and respaced all the time because it needs more space to be nowhere. And its nowhere is a kind of space in which we can all live, finally. Whatever the words are for this space, I cannot say. I mean that: I cannot say, not yet, not now. The language operating in that space all up in the shadows frolics in and as a *field of experience beyond (or, rather, beneath) the constituted reality*.[3] It's where you don't need prior experience for the job because the job can't be done with experience, only with unexperience. It's where we coo and babble, mumble and drivel. It's where the reality we constitute with words unspoken and language unlearned—itself a whole new language to live in—is another reality beneath the other one and without the other one. And we become another we, you another you, I another I. And all of these names become other than what they were, because we have other ones. We have Other names. We have othernames.

We have:

Still, as an adult, long since my initial obsession with them as a child, I am intrigued by shadows. They slather obstructed spaces but are not themselves obstructions. They in fact provide openings. Shadowed places are contingent upon obstructions, unable to exist without being made to by something in the way. Shadows are places that arise when something is in the way.

Have you ever wondered, though, about the possibility of the shadow remaining, of shadowed places remaining, without something in the way? The illegible gender-world I hope for is a shadow realm unobstructed, an unobstructed shadow, a shadow without need for a precipitating obstruction. That is, a dark side that resides on the underside without there being an overside.

What is being asked for is the impossible ability to see the darkness, to see an absence that could deliver us into a new presence. We have long fetishized light. We have beatified its Manichean goodness while attributing to darkness an inherent malady. They say: Light has been our salvation and our guide; light has been our divinity and our pristine afterlife. It is the aim of the quests on which we embark; it never fails us, it is only we who can fail it. Light is infallible, it seems. Light, too, however—on the other hand, the Black-hand side, as it were—is conditioned by an abiding darkness. Light's darkness is an ever-present transgression that undershadows light's bursting exuberance. But it contends of itself that it is always there working. The darkness of light, though given short shrift in appearing center stage (as if it even wanted the assaultive spotlight), is light's surround. Light aims, but its darkness, which always accompanies it as its excessive limits, shrouds. All that the light touches, darkness is the rest. The thing(s) that light is, darkness is everything and nothing else. And there is always more nothing than something.

Why is there something instead of nothing? the old philosophical quip goes. The question itself is misleading. There is both. But nothing is something's infinite excess, its vastness that cannot be conceptualized in language, contingent only on the absence of what we have come to insufficiently call thingness. There is something, which stretches even to metaphysical limits. And then there is nothing, shrouded in and as shadow, which breaches the intelligibility of metaphysical somethingness, wildly ambulating around the pataphysical.

That is a place we can attest to. We frequent it often, listening intimately to the emptiness saturated with everything else. In the beyond, which is right here and has always been, there is a certain subterrain on which life happens. We be there. We can feel it, this subterrain, as it surrounds us without containing us. It is a subterrain that is a vast openness, no pillars or ceilings or floors or walls or locks. An architectural impossibility. That is our architecture. Building more without tools of mastery, a building that happens in our dismantling. In your dismantling. We build down here. It's a lot like up there down here; it's everything that up there cannot be, would not be. So it's not like up there down here; down here can't be that.

Down here we do not dance your dances or speak your language, but therein lies the out that's in here.[4] *What is a dance down here? What is a word, a prayer, a gesture, a life? I cannot say.*

We are a different way, another way for those who need it—and that's everyone, and that's no one. We, down here, give you a way to caress in language those who ill-fit fitting in and get ill when they fit, so that they may finally be what they could not be: what they could not be. So that they may finally be what they could not be: what they have been. So that they may finally be what they could not be:

Hegemonic gender's process—the ways we are formed and inaugurated from without, the ways that y'all tell us what we are permitted to be and how our bodies should move—operates binaristically, slotting unruly subjects into viable social existence by way of legibility. The gendered name bestowed upon us, which is, all in all, more like a branding, claims to speak to something held deeply within, something unique to us and unfettered by our outside. Put paradoxically, this apparent fact said to emanate from us is an already-made badge stabbed into us by someone else. They tell us they call us "boy," call us "girl," because that is what we are, have been, will always be, because there is no outside to this. The violence proliferates; the designation lacks the proper size because what we yearn for are improper sizes that fit us ill-fittingly, it lacks the correct numerical measurements because all we want is to incorrectly measure up. What they've given us, godlike and tyrannical, is a stuffy room with no space to run around in. And they call it viable life.

We are called to speak and ask about the unspeakable and unaskable genders on the outside. We are called to ask to go to the shadows. We will miss the light at first, as it let us see, kept us from bumping into walls; we will want the light's embrace, its luminosity that touted itself as akin to an awakening. The transition will be difficult. But the difficulty is the rub.

A way out resides inside an outside. It is what is slittingly eyeable to me as illegible shadow genders. The tenets of life's viability rest on a fundamental legibility, and this viability rests on having to buy in. Legibility is the price of the proverbial ticket. Punching that ticket has promised wholeness, yet it has dealt us sheer *extimacy*, a determinative engendering from without that bears a hostile relation to the ways we want to leak out. It's coaxed us into pulling that extimacy close, thinking it the intensification of intimacy, but that, we know, was "a hopelessly skewed description." Such an imperious "gift."[5] Illegibility harbors an otherwise that could spin us into another terrain that does not rely on the violent tools given to us. What might it mean and look like, what might it do and feel like, to find viability in illegibility? If we encounter another without the presumption of dictating how they can show up to us, is this illegibility the opening of a pervasive ethical encounter with others?

In the shadows the genders that might become of us lurk. They will not name us, no; naming assumes an inscriptive line of descent, a linear genealogy that affixes our interiority to something outside of us, presuming a knowledge about us that constrains our breadth. We must expand our relations with the illegibility of the shadow and refuse to name, because shadow genders, too dark to abide the contours of names, prefer the unnamed and unnameable in the service of a loving commitment to expansive possibility. If I may try to get at, sideways, what the illegibility of the shadows has in store, what those genders that might be are—those genders that reside in the blackness of it all, reside on the critically intimate dark side—it seems that they exude the possibility of inaugurating our subjectivities through a deregulated ether. In this "black ether," an ungendered gender that exceeds the commandeering norms of violated existence (viable existence as a founding violence), we might give ourselves over in its ether toward a new kind of us. Genders on the run, on the dark side in the Du Boisian "great wandering shadows."[6]

This, I think, is where the dweller in the (under)Commons went when they could not provide their name to my friend, when they could not hear the assaults of the people trying to reel them back here. They could not respond to calls to legibility because shadow genders do not need the light to promise them an existence. They are shadows that roam without needing light to exalt them. These genders are on the move and running as a way to live. Illegibility discontents the normative hubris of our gender dyad, the dyad seeking to send drone strikes on all that threaten its reign. Our shadow genders, though, never get shook 'cause they flee, always, the scene of the crime when the dust settles. Because they are the dust. The scenes they show up at *are* the crime. And criminality, reconfigured and mashed up in the shadows, does not abide the violence of the Law. They will not be subjected to and rendered legible inside the mechanisms churning out the perpetuation of the laws that govern how we are made to fit within the binary. They will traverse the otherwise.

ESCAPE

What will have to be relinquished for us to unleash the imagination's radical creative capacity and draw from it what is needed for the task of thinking The World otherwise? Nothing short of a radical shift in how we approach matter and form.

— Denise Ferreira da Silva, "On Difference
Without Separability"

Flesh Werq

to live
in this flesh is to worship agility,
to call death by its government name.

— Joshua Bennett, "On Extinction"

To fully inhabit the flesh might lead to a different modality
of existence.

— Alexander Weheliye, Habeas Viscus:
Racializing Assemblages, Biopolitics, and
Black Feminist Theories of the Human

    "I would make a distinction in this case between 'body' and 'flesh,'" writes the inimitable Hortense Spillers, my academic mama of sorts, "and impose that distinction as the central one between captive and liberated subject-positions."[1] The body cannot save us; it confines us, keeps us subjected and, indeed, subject to subjection. The body is the scene at which subjection occurs, giving subjection footholds to rummage around in our interiority and damage our valuables. But there is an inherency to our value, interiorized and in need of nothing from without. The flesh, then, is where it's at. We want the flesh, want to live in the flesh, because only there—not in the body's static fixity, its cumbersome anchorage—can we get outside of things and breathe, finally. Breath's expansion is given in the flesh; we can breathe when we werq this flesh.

This flesh is not just mine, or yours; it's ours, we share this flesh and we share in flesh. Coalition happens when we don't presume that we already know each other. Plagued by myths and exclusions, bodies mired in the hubris of cohesion and normalcy can't give us what we need. We need something else, which is why we welcome the flesh in all its coalescing unfastening, its fugitive agency and force of assault on those nets of regulation. Feel the flesh, hear the flesh, Ralph Ellison's lower frequencies when they vibrate beneath lowness.

Putting the flesh to *werq*, claiming an enthusiasm in the expansive capacity of fleshiness to, as they say, make it happen—where "it" is the illegible edge of liberation's horizon—is a potent refusal. *Werqing*, or alternatively *werking*, comes from Black and queer underground socialities, in the hollowed-out buildings, the midnight subway cars, the clandestine balls. It is an affirmative expressive activity used when a way of living "exceed[s] the commonsense of normative categories of social being," when we bring it but bring it new and different.[2] Werqing, because of its love affair with the expressive, the performative, and the affective, is not about that life—or more accurately, that death—of the biological, the documentational, the checked box; werq always happens in the flesh, a different labor in surplus and potential, of repurposing and reworking. Werq is sutured to flesh like a fresh fade on brushed heads, claiming not the rigidity of the body but this ante-body of flesh that we might call that which refuses the body. It takes us through the bowels of "underworlds and undercommons" where things ain't like they used to be. Werqing in the flesh gives us over, because we choose to give ourselves and be given, to "the parasubjective and para-identitarian movement of the labor of werqing it." It's an ecstatic next-to kind of subjectivity, a to-the-side-with-our-backs-turned-to kind of identity. We love it here in this flesh, werqing it, getting werqed by it, giving it werq to do.

Werq, then, is in fact the first right: "an instantiation of a collective negative tendency to differ, to resist the regulative powers that resistance, that differing, call into being."[3] We are different and differently positioned, which demands that we work this thing differently, but in that difference we are working with each other to be with each other on the run. That's where freedom is at, in the escape with our co-conspiratorial escapees. It is the somewhere where summer blooms.

Danez Smith, Black, queer, nonbinary, poz writer and performer, offers flesh space in their poem "summer, somewhere." Without even uttering the word, which is often the only way flesh can be uttered, Smith gifts us with fleshy *poesis*: an illegible making on the run. Reading "summer, somewhere" is an impossible task; it is a treatise, a plea, to not be read. To read it is to perform a kind of unreading, where one learns how to dissolve the grammars that construct the gaze and read askance, read the hieroglyphic scripts illegible to the rest. *Doing* a reading of "summer, somewhere," too, is an impossible task. But I have tried to write that impossibility here, letting it (mis)guide us into another terrain where, indeed, it is summer in a here that is a somewhere.

There, somewhere, where it's summer, we are never dead; we are "alive someplace better."[4] Always life. We dig up those who have been buried and await their smiles. Graves are exhumed and the dead, who were never really dead, ask what took us so long, then sing hymns, rap lyrics, beatbox, croon. They see the sun shining while snow falls, "fall[ing] black," because sun shines even in darkness. Beneath the sky we run as if it were falling, but that's just how we play. And live. And love. We have "afros like maple crowns," like I have, though morning bed-head and constant finger detangling is enough to make you think your hair has it out for you on some follicular vendetta-type shit. Still others of us, others who might be "a heaven of brown / girls" are instead "braiding on golden stoops." Call them cornrows. Call them *plaits*, as my Grandma prefers. Call them micros or call them twists. But call them beautiful too.

Here, somewhere, where it's summer, is where we choose and say our names. Maybe we call each other *ace, G, homie, cuz*. Or we "say our *own* names," in no need of others deemed more alive to recite them for us, in honor of us. We can do it ourselves because we are not dead; we don't die. We won't die. And it is not because we pray—an attempt to call forth absent interlocutors—but because we summon our own shifting shadows, shadows that attest to our presence. We might wander temporarily, for a day, or forever, but we pick our own names, say them, maybe change them, and say them again. There is imaginative epicness there: "O, the imagination of a new reborn boy," Smith writes. What on (or off or beneath or on the outskirts of) Earth might we have at the ready when we don't have to succumb to the legible scripts of what they expect? Well, I can only imagine.

Here, in the flesh, where in somewhere it is summer, "there's no language / for *officer* or *law*, no color to call *white*" because there are no names for chains, no names for capture, no names for violence, no names that we did not fashion for ourselves when we declared that we are still, always, alive. The Law and its minions cannot venture here; here, the summer in somewhere, is just another word for the place where the oppressive force of the Law and all its variegated hues do not dare tread. The only language we have here is one of love, the point of crisis that bursts with and as multiple avenues of shared escape. Somewhere, where we live with flesh, is where we un-be who they said we were (supposed to be). We are not what they said; we are more, so, so much more. Over here, on some real shit, "everybody wanna be black & is." And I think, I hope, Smith means that. We Black over here, where Black is more than *that*. You know what I'm talking about. Black is not and is more than that thing we've been trained to see; it is, maybe, what we can't see (yet), maybe what troubles seeing, maybe what can't be caught in sight. It ain't got no body, and ain't got no mind because it's thoroughly out of its (right) mind. "They" can't see us here or catch us here unless they're here with us, at which point they won't be they anymore but us—together in difference and together to undermine what they were said to have to be too—and we'll be reading with hapticality, hearing with ocularity, smelling with gustation. Illegible hieroglyphics that only we can decipher. Like those of ungendering, unracing, unworlding, or Smith's "unfuneral," which we sometimes do too. It matters less how you got here and more that you're here, werqing. We werq over/down/in here, disinvested, unalienated, nonexploited, uncommodified.

Danez Smith is committed wholeheartedly to expanding the world, never being one for assimilation's siren song, so they write expansive geographies onto the page, what Katherine McKittrick would deem "black geographies"—the ~~inverse obverse~~ subverse of the seemingly "predetermined stabilities, such as boundaries, color-lines, 'proper' places, fixed and settled infrastructures and streets"[5]—and ask a most poignant question: "do you know what it's like to live / on land who loves you back." Land *who* loves you back, not land *that* loves you back. Land is sentient, with subjective personhood. Land is a *who*, not a *that* or an *it*. Capable of loving too. The tentative answer to the question of loving land and land-loving is the eradication of geography, of making maps and map-making, because, as we know thanks to Sylvia Wynter, we always unjustly mistake the map for the rhizomatic complexity of the territory. There is, for Smith, no longer "a need for geography / now" beneath the summer in somewhere, because "we safe everywhere." When we are safe over here, up in the flesh, fearing nothing. That's freedom. Ask Nina Simone.

In summery flesh we are "dancing between the storm" because the binary poles are always stormy, never letting up with their torrents. So we make life between them, somewhere unlocatable because *between* is not a place per se, just an approximation of uncaptured motion. Our werq is a dance. Please, I implore you, reader, "don't call / us dead, call us alive someplace better"—in the flesh, putting it to werq.

Flesh werqin' is at base—a baseless base pissed off with the fixity of basedness (and its connotative militancy)—a fugitive flesh, which is and must be, further, "gender self-determination, queer abolition, and trans resistance."[6] It is both the fleshiness of those who have taken to the mischievous and enlivening plight of being bad and a stepping into runaway flesh, engendering one's oneness in a fundamental not-oneness. The werqin' is unwieldy, volatile, *assemblic*—complex and shifty arrangements and disarrangements of content networks. Assemblages of flesh, or the subjectivities that congeal when we, over and over, do flesh werq, put pressure on our most fundamental ways of knowing, ways that are tethered to hegemony. Flesh werq, then, is queer in the sense that it interrupts the violence of the normative that attends gendered enforcements, sexual norms, particularly as it pertains to and is inflected by the disruption and trouble that is Blackness. Flesh werq makes forms of control, gender chief among them, spaz out. And in this spazzing, we suspend the violence that betides us. We-on-the-run-together, which is the place where we can be together.

There is a question of how we exist with one another, how and what we *see* when we encounter those with whom we cohabit in the social world. How and what we see is an ethical demand placed on us when we encounter others. Representation matters, for sure. The quotable cliché has long served us well: we can't be what we can't see. I question, though, in a timid gesture of interrogation, whether the world in which we live, the structures in play that structure how we play, has the capacity to produce an "accurate" representation of our subjectivity, particularly the subjectivity of those who are marginalized. What of Black women in the prevailing structure's gaze, a structural gaze that has as its goal to do everything it can to not see that irruptive nexus of Black and woman? Entering the interrogation of these circumstances via Black feminism, we might assert that "the coherence and specificity of black female subjects"—subjects who break optics, deviant and runaway subjects who can't and won't be contained—"is effaced by the logic that cannot produce her positionality except paradoxically."[7] Representational logics are hegemonic ones, logics that rely on linear input-output and zero-ones, inept with the quantum polysemy of the Black, the woman, the queer, the on-the-run-from being. They in here coming at us sideways and cop attitudes when they catch the side-eye. You can only come at me wrong if you don't have the tools necessary to come at me at all. So we look to the flesh, work it and werq it, to get its feel, its fecundity, its escapeful pirouette. We know that it's mad hard to assuage the embodied plight of various forms of material, ideological, and social oppression. But to neither have nor be flesh, to instead werq it joyously and openly, noncovetously so everybody else can get in on it, is to engage the surplus of that violence and, at the same time, claim the emanating liveliness in its flight, its aspirations of freedom, its possibility. Put crassly, if we're all fucked, if this world is fucked, if all this shit is pretty much fucked, it is necessary for us not to concede that this is the end. We might be fucked, but we will not stay that way. We can keep working, working in the flesh because to live in the flesh is life, impossible life that's lively as all hell, after we exceed the bareness of abjection. Surely the flesh was violated into the body (the body as violated flesh) via whips, chains, slurs, fists, institutions, discourses, assault rifles, angry mobs, and, and, and. . . . Flesh, though, is never entirely exterminated; flesh is hidden, never wiped out. And this enables the persistent possibility of an otherwise body, an otherwise knowledge, an otherwise history that moonwalks on the edges just out of the bounds of domination. How do we refuse this subjugation even as we come into a kind of social being precisely through subjugation? How do we revise how we "show up" in order to come into being in excess of the terroristic logics of being itself? We know ourselves as ourselves, in part, because various legible frameworks commanded by power give us slim pickin's as to what they will allow to exist. Okay, that's cool. We don't want none of that, nothing they got. What we choose is the flesh.

The tradition we must choose is one of possibility. Even in the impossible there is a graspable glimmer that propels us to get working on this freedom. Possibility as emancipatory. They don't love our flesh over here 'cause they can't think outside and outdoors, out-to-the-side and out-of-doors. If they can't love our flesh over here we might have to get moving. And in the moving we love flesh, hug flesh and let it hug us back, a hug that sets us flitting. That's where love is: in the divergence from where they don't, and can't, love your moving outside. We wild and wildin' because we are werqin' this flesh that has always been here, always ledgered memory's mnemonic discontent. Flesh remains, always, here to inhabit and move in between. We might not have kinfolk, we might not have language or property, documentation or riches, but in the absence of all'a'dat we still have flesh: flesh that, if werqed, lives and speaks and feels and imagines.

We get displaced when we inhabit the flesh. In that displacement we are all up in dis place, in a new kind of social world, living, loving, and thinking on the outside, ante-sovereign. No, you don't gotta go to work, but you do gotta put in werq. And it'll sound melodious too, be soundin' like a singsongy wail from a fugitive's harp alerting everyone else who's on the run, a song on the low for those on the sneak. I can't tell you how many songs I done heard that made me think my flesh'd get up and crawl off to a spot no one knew about and just hum to itself without the pretense of sounding like humming. That's a different kind of apparatus, a different kind of instrument, one whose unregulated movement is a radical rethinking of how we might get outside of ourselves, outside of who we (never) are. Flesh is always getting outside and being inside the outside. It just works like that because we werq it like that.

Defy degradation and exhaust suppressive description, flesh, while remaining ungraspable even when touching. Flesh sings to us, it sings *from* us and beckons us to come into it. A musical moment, but a moment that does not reside between start and finish; a musical moment that rhythmically already has happened and is already happening—that's what we mean by *happ'nin'*—because there are folks at the party who've been jumping for a minute, working the fleshiness of an unwrought and unbought labor, feasting on how this all facilitates healing. These folks are experimenting with pipettes and Erlenmeyer flasks of a different breed. They don't measure or quantify but embrace openly, radically open in a treacherous teetering between life and that life that could kill you, refusing to demand that anyone show up in a way that adheres to conventional optics, and instead demanding only that you be given in the flesh, insurgent, incalculable, ungovernable.

The flesh is filled with dragons. "Here be dragons" comes from the historically used Latin phrase "HC SVNT DRACONES" (i.e., *hic sunt dracones*, "here are dragons"), in reference to the medieval practice of drawing dragons, serpents, and other mythological creatures in uncharted cartographical territories to designate an area as dangerous. The flesh is uncharted, dragon-filled, illegibly unpredictable. We don't do lines, we amble in peripatetic movement not only geographical but ideological, internal, syntactic, and ontological. Werqed flesh, fugitive flesh, para-possesses—in a tense "open relationship" with covetous possession, in the gap between holding and having—a ludic dimension; that is, a disposition garnered through a playful act of assemblage, thrusting us into a slipstream world that is other than other, in defiance of the demand to categorize.

I want alternative modes of life under and outside of the definitional power of the State. I want that "*insurgent* ground" that my academic mama yearns for, that claimed monstrosity that might be the radical nonmessianic salvation we wish to be living here, or somewhere, but here nonetheless. To live in and with flesh, in the language of Joshua Bennett's epigraph at the outset of this meditation, is to *worship agility*. Evading death, calling it by its government name, an egregious offense if there ever was one. But that's how much we get going—not even death is welcome here in the flesh, the werq too joyous, too effusive to be captured by its necrophilic tendrils. We don't capture the flesh; it gives us the life we sought. Somewhere, a somewhere *in which we can be defiant, together, unabashedly alive.*[8] Mobilize those witchy flights, the seething astral specter that hopes for, without knowing its contours in advance, a more radical else*here* populated by those fugitively Black and radically ungendered subjectivities with whom we might commune.

When we put the flesh to werq in the service of motion and evasion from capture, there's no need for fear. "[D]on't fret," Danez Smith says, because somewhere in flesh werq "we don't die."

Laying in the Cut

Lay in the cut like they not gon' know
'cause if I gotta make a move, dawg, they not gon' know.

— Mos Def, "Close Edge"

Torkwase Dyson's art emancipates the captive from captivity; her art, ranging from paintings that ooze with ecological rebellion to sculptures that manifest the curvature of compositional thought, can make concrete bleed a sable color so rich with vibrancy that to gaze upon it is to be shrouded in riotous onyx. Dyson, born in Chicago and raised between North Carolina and Mississippi, paints through distilled geometric abstraction and creates idiosyncratic diagrams and expressive languages. Her brushstrokes refashion how space is known and encountered, or re-known and given over to us, through the residue and traces of it all. She improvises, which is to say she is given over from somewhere else, in an exploratory artistic rap session with how we arrange and disarrange ourselves in (dis)order to move through the world.

The installation *In Plane Site* is tellingly subtitled *Fugitive*. Its components, most notably the piece "Black Interiority," are meant to explore what Dyson calls "architecture of emancipations," considering how we negotiate and negate systems and systemic order as a means to cultivate autonomy. What she is building with her art is emancipatory space—space that, in short, is free and freeing. What Dyson commits to is "an unfixed set of relationships," relationships that dissolve tethers and fashion new ones because they are not cemented in determined ways. Her work "refuses . . . fixed systems in favor of a responsiveness to new potential, reconfiguration and exchange."[1] We cannot and will not be fixed; we are not broken nor will we sit still like obstinate children scolded by parents. Let childish obstinacy, curiosity, and mischief proliferate; let the Blackness of our interiority do its reconfigurative work in response to being accosted by evils, oppressed by power, dissed by the world, and even nothing at all—just for the hell of it.

Responding to the tragedies of those in captivity—Anthony Burns, who literally shipped himself to freedom; Henry "Box" Brown, who captured himself in a box in order to mail himself to freedom; Harriet Jacobs, who confined herself to a crawl space for seven years as a means of evasion—"Black Interiority" displaces captivity, refashions it, werqs it, creating capacity within and in excess of captivity. Mined are the clandestine politics of self-emancipation, politicized stolen life. Extracted and abstracted is Dyson's "subversive ability to escape," her practice of refusal, her mood of fugitivity.

Dyson's architectural emancipatory artistry indexes a fugitivity interested in, as I am, how the space of lawlessness imagines in excess of the crevice carved out by means of one's practice of refusal. Fugitivity's escape does not presume a known location, nor does it presume that getting outside of where it's at won't lead to another getting outside of where *that's* at. Its heft is in its disavowal of what we've been given coupled with an embrace of an unknowable something else. The imaginative space, the emancipatory architecture, is fugitivity's fuel, without us knowing what might come to inhabit that architecture. The imaginative space, like one of Dyson's 2018 acrylics on canvas, is "Otherwise."

What this seems to imply about a tradition of escape from captivity is a steadfast will to life and living. What in fact would life be if I wasn't thinking about how I inhabit the world as this being that I am always, ruthlessly, becoming in excess of what I am said to be; this being that exists in volatility betwixt and between governing forces trying to limn my fissures, that dramatizes from the interstices of the order that proclaims itself pure? What would I be thinking if I wasn't thinking about how to live?

It is life that threads me, threads us, I think. Life, which is so often goaded by malicious means into nonlife yet persists anyway. Life is obstinate. Life is unruly, always shrugging off that thanatoid noise. Life is a grandmother with food already out for you, making sure you ain't getting skinny. Life is those quiet moments, quiet even amid the girthy decibels of the world, when we choose again and again, forever and ever, to be here, and to become again.

It's from that will to life that we must do the work we do. I am tired of mourning, though mourning most definitely makes the claim that the exterminated are indeed lives worth grieving. Nevertheless, I am tired of rallying only when we have one, two, nine, forty-nine fewer. They become useful to us only when they can no longer be useful to themselves. I don't want that. I don't want that.

I don't want that.

I want an obstinately fugitive Black feminism that refuses to concede to the categorical truth of things staying as they are, indeed of things staying as they are presumed to always have to be. I want a fugitive Black feminism that has as its bedrock a powerful imagination capable of envisioning what is not, and has never been, the case, *but must be.*

I want life, all of it, and I want it celebrated. Come on, y'all, *come celebrate / with me that everyday / something has tried to kill me / and has failed.*[2] It's in the living that we do the damn thing. Know that the dead are often etched onto concrete slabs amid decomposing flesh all too soon, and know that they indeed lived lives worth shedding tears for. Know, too, and perhaps primarily, that we still here, we still in this, we still live precisely because of the things they tried to kill us for, and we still live because others have sent us running with our lives. Even as we are shot in the back, we say, as we fall, to keep running, our captured-but-never-captured being on the run allowing someone else to keep running, a running that has been given in excess of failed attempts to completely stanch our running. They tryna kill us, but we got no time for that, no time for them and their murderous fancies because we are too busy over here living. We live, as we've been doing this whole time, showing our teeth, not knowing if we're smiling or foreshadowing an onslaught. Often it's both. Even more often it's neither, because we ain't got time to fret over them. This is ours. Our life is our sea, churning and letting us float across the instability.

We make our moves from life; it's where we begin and end our work. It is where we can and must do coalition. Sometimes we don't even know how to stay alive, only that we desirously want to. But if we are to devise a way to live harder, to simply live, it is in coalitional work—gritty, difficult, monstrous work—that this might happen. Grabbing and cherishing more accomplices, bringing in more folks on the grounds of their willingness to get in the trenches with you, is what happens in coalitional work. It's Tommy Pickles with a screwdriver capable of getting free of any playpen(itentiary). Some might think that the new folks who haven't always been in our "barred rooms" might try to kill us—as if they even could!—but, for sure, we bring them in "because that's the only way you can figure you can stay alive." This is a coalitional politics that is ready to lace up the kicks, strap on the gloves, and get to it, a coalitional politics the likes of Bernice Johnson Reagan's homegirlish Black feminism:

> It must become necessary for all of us to feel that this is our world. And that we are here to stay and that anything that is here is ours to take and to use in our image. And watch that "our"—*make it as big as you can*—it ain't got nothing to do with that barred room [where there are

only folks that look like you]. The "our" must include everybody you have to include in order for you to survive. . . . Cause I ain't gonna let you live unless you let me live. Now there's danger in that, but there's also the possibility that we can both live—if you can stand it.[3]

The love in this, the yearning to expand who our people be and how we are to get it poppin'. Reagan's Black feminist coalitional politics means that here in this coalition we go by different rules. We go by the ways of the goons, the ways of the fugitive, the ways of a tradition that's always been cut from the cloth—no, that's *been the cut* of the cloth. We can live in the cut. The coalition's goons are in the cut.

That interiority, that free and freeing space of emancipatory architecture, is a cut in the tapestry. If we are cut from the same cloth, as they say, then some of us were lost at the place that was cut. That cut place, the width of a hair's edge, harbors those of us who now lie there cookin' up schemes. Indeed, the cut is precisely where Black life, feminist life, trans life, queer life resides. A kind of undercommons where subversive intellectuals dwell, the cut resounds with the myriad ways we don't die or stay dead even when they try to kill us. Mos Def's epigraph engenders for me a way of thinking fugitivity as an unintelligible knowledge-making in the unknowingness of knowability. We lay in the cut, escaped from the legible terrain of what was or what supervenes on the knownness of bodying gestures. Lay in, and imagine otherwise, the cut, because the cut is possibility; it is possibility, of course, which is to say life living other than and in excess of its myopic circumscription. In the cut we move against and outside of, beyond and beneath, sovereignty. Can you see us, feel us, hear us, catch us? Nah. Over here, and under here, where *we* be at—a *we* that is a burly, multiplicitous, heterogeneous goon (*I go by them goon rules* . . . .) that, as Mos Def says, "pull[s] up to your spot on low"—is all up in the cut, refusing to succumb, struggling, loving, living. And it is here that we "gotta make [our] move, dawg," because these are the fugitive movements that can't be tracked ("they not gon' know"). The emergence of our fugitive impulses will not be known by the proverbial "they"; our moves of fugitivity will go under, over, across, and beyond the radar. And it is our movement, only the movement, that constitutes the knowing that they not gon', and can't, know.

When I am asked the question my brother, in his I'm-too-cool-for-this-shit vocal inflection, often asks upon seeing me—"Yo, Quis, what's good witchu?"—I think the only appropriate response is to laugh. "Hahahaha." I hope that my words, my language, have revealed something urgent and substantive to you, reader. An urgency and substance that marks the fuzzy, cacophonously symphonic texture of goon rules. It is my hope—perhaps even a plea, or a demand—that the name, like the artful escape of the fugitive, lies just to the side of your fixating interpretive gaze.

Though hegemonic forces structure our horizons, our very being, the texture of our inhabitation of (or violent exclusion from) the world, they cannot and do not determine these things. We can do, and have long done, what we were not supposed to within the structures in force; we can be and have been bad subjects insofar as who we've been told we have to be—not by any means the only subjectivity by which we can live—has been, despite everything, refused in favor of something else. Though we are told to be miserable, to be nothing, to remain fixed in abjection, we can, like the mythical Sisyphus, imagine ourselves otherwise. When he played tricks on the gods, mocking their omnipotent divinity, Sisyphus's levity and disdain for oppressive control landed him a fate believed to be impenetrably bleak. Sisyphus was condemned by the gods to, for eternity, perform the ceaseless task of rolling a boulder up, up, up a mountain only to have it tumble back down, awaiting another round. All because Sisyphus stole divine secrets and put Death in chains. He was, at base, one who loved life. And for this, Sisyphus was condemned to futile and hopeless labor, an unbreachable abjection for his fugitive machinations. Or so they thought. They thought that scorning the gods, despising death, and loving life demanded that one be punished with a ceaseless task resulting in nothing; they thought that this was the ultimate punishment and display of unyielding sovereignty over the fates of mortals. Nevertheless, Sisyphus negates the gods and escapes even their reach. He concludes, in the face of it all, that it is the struggle that conjures joy, that serving without a master in the face of divine mastery is where the liveliest of life happens. His descent, after watching the boulder—that great rock—beckon him from the bottom, is a radically open playground of incendiary thoughts: he is, after all, still that trickster he was punished for being in the first place. The gods cannot punish those thoughts or what he commits to scheming on his descent; the lives we might live in excess of this oppressive regime and all its nefarious tentacles happen in our descent back toward the cackling boulder. And we, clandestinely, boldly, cackle back.

NOTES

Preface

1. Thomas Paine, *Common Sense* (Philadelphia: W. and T. Bradford, 1776).

Whence We Are Sent

1. Javon Johnson, "Black and Happy," 2016.
2. Mikhail Bakhtin, *The Dialogic Imagination: Four Essays*, ed. Michael Holquist, trans. Caryl Emerson (1975; repr., Austin: University of Texas Press, 1983).
3. Andrew Robinson, "In Theory Bakhtin: Dialogism, Polyphony and Heteroglossia," *Ceasefire Magazine*, July 29, 2011, https://ceasefiremagazine .co.uk/in-theory-bakhtin-1/.
4. W. E. B. Du Bois, *The Souls of Black Folk: Essays and Sketches* (Chicago: A. C. McClurg & Co., 1903).

Them Goon Rules

1. Mos Def, "Mathematics," *Black on Both Sides*, Rawkus / Priority Records, 1999.
2. Fred Moten, "The Case of Blackness," *Criticism* 50, no. 2 (Spring 2008): 177–218.
3. Morgan Parker, "Afro," in *There Are More Beautiful Things Than Beyoncé* (Portland, OR; New York: Tin House Books, 2017).

4. Claudia Rankine, *Citizen: An American Lyric* (Minneapolis: Graywolf Press, 2014).

5. Stefano Harney and Fred Moten, *The Undercommons: Fugitive Planning & Black Study* (Wivenhoe: Minor Compositions, 2013).

6. J. Kameron Carter, "Paratheological Blackness," *South Atlantic Quarterly* 112, no. 4 (October 1, 2013): 589–611.

7. Fred Moten, "Blackness and Nothingness (Mysticism in the Flesh)," *South Atlantic Quarterly* 112, no. 4 (October 1, 2013): 737–80.

8. Moten, "Blackness and Nothingness."

9. Cathy J. Cohen, "Punks, Bulldaggers, and Welfare Queens: The Radical Potential of Queer Politics?," *GLQ: A Journal of Lesbian and Gay Studies* 3, no. 4 (January 1, 1997): 437–65.

10. Aesop Rock, "Zero Dark Thirty," *Skelethon*, Rhymesayers Entertainment, 2012; Aesop Rock, "Daylight," *Labor Days*, Definitive Jux, 2002.

11. Christina Sharpe, *In the Wake: On Blackness and Being* (Durham, N.C.: Duke University Press, 2016).

12. Jared Sexton, "Ante-Anti-Blackness: Afterthoughts," *Lateral* no. 1 (2012), http://csalateral.org/section/theory/ante-anti-blackness-afterthoughts -sexton/.

13. Sarah Jane Cervenak, "'Black Night Is Falling': The 'Airy Poetics' of Some Performance," *TDR / The Drama Review* 62, no. 1 (2018): 166–69.

On Being Called a Thug

1. All quotations in this paragraph are from Denise Riley, *Impersonal Passion: Language as Affect* (Durham, N.C.: Duke University Press, 2005).

Dawg Fights

1. Harney and Moten, *The Undercommons*.

The ALP Journals

1. Jared Sexton, "People-of-Color-Blindness: Notes on the Afterlife of Slavery," *Social Text* 28, no. 2 (June 1, 2010): 31–56.

2. C. Riley Snorton, *Black on Both Sides: A Racial History of Trans Identity* (Minneapolis: University of Minnesota Press, 2017).

3. Combahee River Collective, "The Combahee River Collective Statement (1977)," in *How We Get Free: Black Feminism and the Combahee*

River Collective, ed. Keeanga-Yamahtta Taylor (Chicago: Haymarket Books, 2017). Emphasis mine.

4. All quotations in this paragraph are from Eric A. Stanley, "Gender Self-Determination," *TSQ: Transgender Studies Quarterly* 1, no. 1/2 (January 1, 2014): 89–90.

5. Michelle O'Brien, "Gender Skirmishes on the Edges: Notes on Gender Identity, Self-Determination and Anticolonial Struggle," *Anarcha Library* (blog), 2003, http://anarchalibrary.blogspot.com/2010/09 /gender-skirmishes-on-edges-notes-on.html.

6. Sora Han, "Abolition: At Issue, In Any Case," *Lateral* no. 3 (2014), http:// csalateral.org/issue3/theory/han. Emphasis mine.

7. Judith Butler, "Reply from Judith Butler to Mills and Jenkins," *Differences* 18, no. 2 (January 1, 2007): 180–95.

8. Andrea Gibson, *Pansy: A Collection of Poetry* (Austin, Tex.: Write Bloody Publishing, 2015).

9. Kathi Weeks, "Introduction: The Politics of the Public Toilet," *South Atlantic Quarterly* 115, no. 4 (October 1, 2016): 744–47.

10. Che Gossett, "Žižek's Trans/Gender Trouble," *Los Angeles Review of Books*, September 13, 2016, https://lareviewofbooks.org/article/zizeks -transgender-trouble/#!.

11. Amanda Armstrong, "Certificates of Live Birth and Dead Names: On the Subject of Recent Anti-Trans Legislation," *South Atlantic Quarterly* 116, no. 3 (July 2017): 621–31.

Three Theses

1. Moten, "Case of Blackness"; Ashon T. Crawley, *Blackpentecostal Breath: The Aesthetics of Possibility* (New York: Fordham University Press, 2017).

2. Toni Morrison, "Unspeakable Things Unspoken: The Afro-American Presence in American Literature," *Michigan Quarterly Review* 28 (1988): 1–34.

3. Fred Moten, "Black Op," *PMLA* 123, no. 5 (2008): 1743–47.

4. Alexis Pauline Gumbs, "Evidence," in *Octavia's Brood: Science Fiction Stories from Social Justice Movements*, ed. Walidah Imarisha, adrienne maree brown, and Sheree Renée Thomas (Oakland: AK Press, 2015), 33–42.

5. Zora Neale Hurston, "How It Feels to Be Colored Me," *The World Tomorrow*, June 1928.

6. Hortense J. Spillers, *Black, White, and in Color: Essays on American Literature and Culture* (Chicago: University of Chicago Press, 2003); Toni Morrison, "No Place for Self-Pity, No Room for Fear," *The Nation*, March 23, 2015, https://www.thenation.com/article/no-place-self-pity-no-room-fear/; Jessica Stern, "This Is What Pride Looks Like: Miss Major and the Violence, Poverty, and Incarceration of Low-Income Transgender Women," *S&F Online: The Scholar & Feminist Online* 10, no. 1/2 (2011).

7. Tina Campt, "Black Feminist Futures and the Practice of Fugitivity" (Helen Pond McIntyre '48 Lecture, Barnard Center for Research on Women, October 7, 2014). Emphasis mine.

8. All quotations in this paragraph are from Cohen, "Punks, Bulldaggers, and Welfare Queens."

9. Kai M. Green, "'Race and Gender Are Not the Same!' Is Not a Good Response to the 'Transracial'/Transgender Question OR We Can and Must Do Better," *The Feminist Wire*, June 14, 2015, http://www.thefeministwire.com/2015/06/race-and-gender-are-not-the-same-is-not-a-good-response-to-the-transracial-transgender-question-or-we-can-and-must-do-better/.

10. Kai M. Green, "Troubling the Water: Mobilizing a Trans* Analytic," in *No Tea, No Shade: New Writings in Black Queer Studies*, ed. E. Patrick Johnson (Durham, N.C.: Duke University Press, 2016), 65–81.

11. Lyndon K. Gill, "Representing Freedom: Diaspora and the Meta-Queerness of Dub Theater," in *No Tea, No Shade: New Writings in Black Queer Studies*, ed. E. Patrick Johnson (Durham, N.C.: Duke University Press, 2016), 113–30.

12. Denise Riley, *"Am I That Name?": Feminism and the Category of "Women" in History* (London: Macmillan Press, 1988).

13. James Baldwin, "Everybody's Protest Novel," in *The Price of the Ticket: Collected Nonfiction, 1948–1985* (New York: St. Martin's / Marek, 1985).

A Series of (Un)related Events

1. Claudia Rankine, *Citizen: An American Lyric* (Minneapolis, MN: Graywolf Press, 2014).

2. Joshua Bennett, "Still Life with Black Death," 2015.

3. Robin Tremblay-McGaw, "Enclosure and Run: The Fugitive Recyclopedia of Harryette Mullen's Writing," *MELUS* 35, no. 2 (Summer 2010): 73.

4. All quotations in this paragraph are from Sarah Jane Cervenak, *Wandering: Philosophical Performances of Racial and Sexual Freedom* (Durham, N.C.: Duke University Press, 2014).

5. Saidiya Hartman, "The Belly of the World: A Note on Black Women's Labors," *Souls* 18, no. 1 (March 14, 2016): 166–73.

6. Gloria Anzaldúa, "How to Tame a Wild Tongue," in *Out There: Marginalization and Contemporary Cultures*, ed. Russell Ferguson, Martha Gever, Trinh T. Minh-ha, and Cornel West (Cambridge, Mass.: MIT Press, 1990), 203–11.

7. Reina Gossett, "An Open Letter for Gender Self-Determination in/at OWS," *Post Post Script*, December 2011.

8. Fred Moten and Stefano Harney, "From Cooperation to Black Operation: A Conversation with Stefano Harney and Fred Moten on *The Undercommons*," Transversal Texts, April 2016, http://transversal.at/blog/From-cooperation-to-black-operation.

Scenes of Illegible Shadow Genders

1. Eula Biss, "The Pain Scale," *Creative Nonfiction* 1, no. 32 (2007): 65–84.

2. Karla FC Holloway, *Legal Fictions: Constituting Race, Composing Literature* (Durham, N.C.: Duke University Press, 2013).

3. Gilles Deleuze, "Immanence: Une vie . . . ," quoted in John Marks, *Gilles Deleuze: Vitalism and Multiplicity* (London: Pluto Press, 1998).

4. Lisa Capretto, "Dr. Maya Angelou: 'Be a Rainbow in Somebody Else's Cloud,'" *Huffington Post*, May 30, 2014, video, https://www.huffington post.com/2014/05/30/maya-angelou-oprah-rainbow_n_5413544.html.

5. Riley, *Impersonal Passion*.

6. J. Kameron Carter and Sarah Jane Cervenak, "Black Ether," *CR: The New Centennial Review* 16, no. 2 (2016): 203–24; Du Bois, *Souls of Black Folk*.

Flesh Werq

1. Hortense J. Spillers, "Mama's Baby, Papa's Maybe: An American Grammar Book," *Diacritics* 17, no. 2 (July 1, 1987): 65–81.

2. All quotations in this paragraph are from Treva Ellison, "The Labor of Werqing It: The Performance and Protest Strategies of Sir Lady Java," in *Trap Door: Trans Cultural Production and the Politics of Visibility*, ed. Reina Gossett, Eric A. Stanley, and Johanna Burton, Critical Anthologies in Art and Culture (Cambridge, Mass.: MIT Press, 2017), 1–22.

3. Fred Moten, "Black Optimism / Black Operation" (lecture, Chicago, October 19, 2007), https://www.scribd.com/document/182136484/Moten -Fred-Black-Optimism-Black-Operation-doc.

4. This and subsequent quotations are from Danez Smith, "summer, some-where," in *Don't Call Us Dead: Poems* (Minneapolis: Graywolf Press, 2017), 3–24.

5. Katherine McKittrick, *Demonic Grounds: Black Women and the Cartog-raphies of Struggle* (Minneapolis: University of Minnesota Press, 2006).

6. Eric A. Stanley, "Introduction: Fugitive Flesh: Gender Self-Determination, Queer Abolition, and Trans Resistance," in *Captive Genders: Trans Embod-iment and the Prison Industrial Complex*, ed. Eric A. Stanley and Nat Smith (Oakland: AK Press, 2011), 1–11.

7. Jennifer DeVere Brody, "Effaced into Flesh: Black Women's Subjec-tivity," in *On Your Left: The New Historical Materialism*, ed. Ann M. Kibbey, Thomas Foster, Carol Siegel, and Ellen Berry (New York: NYU Press, 1996), 184–205.

8. Joshua Bennett, "I Juke the Apocalypse: Teaching 'Gravity,'" *Muzzle*, November 27, 2015, https://www.muzzlemagazine.com/vital-signs/6 -joshua-bennett-on-gravity-by-angel-nafis.

Laying in the Cut

1. Torkwase Dyson, "First painting I finished in 2017," Instagram, Janu-ary 1, 2018, https://www.instagram.com/p/BdaUi7xg_h5/.

2. Lucille Clifton, "Won't You Celebrate with Me," in *Collected Poems of Lucille Clifton* (Rochester, N.Y.: BOA Editions, 1992).

3. Bernice Johnson Reagan, "Coalition Politics: Turning the Century," in *Home Girls: A Black Feminist Anthology*, ed. Barbara Smith (New Brunswick, N.J.: Rutgers University Press, 1983).

ABOUT THE AUTHOR

Marquis Bey is a PhD candidate in English at Cornell University. He has received fellowships from Humanities New York and the Ford Foundation.